BEYOND JUST WIN

The Story of G.A. Moore
Texas High School Football's No. 1 Coach

Ed Housewright

BLUE RIVER PRESS

Indianapolis, Indiana

Beyond Just Win

Published by Blue River Press
Indianapolis, Indiana
www.brpressbooks.com

Distributed by Cardinal Publishers Group
Tom Doherty Company, Inc.
www.cardinalpub.com

ISBN: 978-1-68157-009-9

Author: Ed Housewright
Editor: Morgan Sears
Interior Design: Dave Reed
Cover Design: David Miles
Cover Photograph: Phil Bailiff
Interior Photos Courtesy of G.A. Moore unless otherwise noted

Printed in the United States of America

Dedication

To my son, Connor,
who has grown into a fine young man.
I'm very proud of you.

Contents

Author's Note

G.A. Moore intrigued me for years.

As a Dallas native and a reporter for the *Dallas Morning News*, I had heard about Moore's success as football coach in the small North Texas towns of Celina and Pilot Point. Newspaper accounts talked about his phenomenal winning record and string of state championships. They also alluded to the extreme devotion he inspired in players and townspeople.

In 2012, after I left the newspaper, I decided to find out what made this coach so special. I called Moore, and he was receptive to the idea of a book on his life. We began meeting regularly for long talks in his modest home on two hundred acres that have been in his family for more than a century. After interviewing him, I turned my attention to scores of former players who learned football – and life lessons – under Moore from the early 1960s through 2011.

I heard remarkable stories of leadership and service. Players recalled how Moore demanded perfection and pushed them to reach their potential as individuals and teammates. He pushed but he also encouraged. I never heard a story of Moore verbally or physically abusing a player. He was stern but supportive – without exception. On the field, Moore instructed players on the finer points of the game. Off the field, he made sure they respected their teachers, obeyed their parents, and lived by a moral compass.

Winning coaches sometimes have a dark side. They may have a massive ego, a mean streak, or a dismissive attitude toward others. Moore has none of those. He's inspired numerous former players to follow his footsteps into coaching. The man who succeeded Moore as head coach in Celina played for him and coached under him for twenty-five years.

Moore developed a leadership style that coaches in Celina, Pilot Point, and elsewhere follow, yet he had a singular identity. How many coaches invite players to their home to go swimming? How many teach them how to bale hay and rope calves? How many host Fellowship of Christian Athletes meetings and encourage teenagers to find their own faith? How many coaches befriend students who have no interest in football? Moore did.

He became a mentor, a father figure, and a friend to two generations of players. His story offers valuable lessons for anyone interested in motivating people, building a successful organization, and developing character.

Now in his seventies, Moore's coaching days are over. His legacy, however, continues as former players follow his example of excellence and pass on his message to future generations. It was a joy to get to know Coach G.A. Moore.

***

A few words about the book's organization: Chapter 1 gives an overview of Coach Moore's achievements, influence, and personality. Chapters 2 through 6 recount his coaching stints in Pilot Point, Celina, and Aubrey. Chapter 7 describes a handful of people who were influenced in memorable ways by Moore. Chapter 8 details the rich history and appeal of Texas high school football, highlighting a number of successful coaches who preceded Moore. Chapter 9, the final one, covers Moore's post-football life today that finds him pastoring – and reviving – a small country church.

At the end of each chapter, I have a section called *"In His Own Words..."* Here, the highly quotable Moore talks about subjects close to his heart. He explains how to motivate young players and unite communities. He recalls his experiences growing up on a farm and playing high school and college football. He discusses the importance of faith and family in his life. Moore's unique expressions and insights reveal a larger-than-life but humble man who left an extraordinary legacy.

Foreword

By Lovie Smith

I've admired G.A. Moore since I was in high school four decades ago.

In 1974, my Big Sandy High School Wildcats faced Coach Moore's Celina High School Bobcats for the Class B Texas High School championship. We had a team bursting with talent. Players such as David Overstreet, an all-state running back who starred at the University of Oklahoma and became a first-round NFL draft pick; and myself, an all-state linebacker and two-time All-American at the University of Tulsa.

But Celina, while not blessed with the same natural talent as Big Sandy, played with heart and discipline, and that started with G.A. Moore. Coach Moore created a brilliant defensive strategy that suffocated our high-octane offense. We battled to a 0-0 tie in an epic defensive struggle to share the state title.

Since that game, I've followed Coach Moore's career from afar. While my own coaching career has taken me from Texas middle school to the National Football League, Coach Moore chose to remain at the high school level. I admire him for that. With his knowledge of the game and motivational abilities, he could have succeeded as a college or professional coach, but Coach Moore found his calling inspiring young men. All great coaches are teachers first and foremost, and Coach Moore taught his players how to win in both football and in life.

A man of great faith and humility, Coach Moore won more high school football games than anyone in Texas history – an extraordinary accomplishment. More

importantly, he molded young men into exemplary con-
tributors to society, and he unified towns around their
shared love of Texas high school football.

I was honored to share the stage with Coach Moore when
we were inducted into the Texas Sports Hall of Fame in
2012. When Coach Moore stepped to the microphone for
his acceptance speech, dozens of former players, coaching
colleagues, and supporters rose to their feet and gave him
an extended ovation. The reception showed the enormous
respect and love people hold for G.A. Moore. His legacy
cannot be overstated; he set a sky-high standard for all
coaches – and for anyone else interested in influencing
people.

BEYOND JUST WIN

Chapter 1
<u>The Winningest Coach</u>

G.A. Moore has good reason to boast, if he were the boasting type.

In a forty-five year coaching career, he won more games than anyone in the storied history of Texas high school football. No other state can match the level of competition and intensity found in the Lone Star State, the undisputed hotbed of high school football. Few coaches can field a championship-caliber team year after year – and yet Moore did.

He compiled a record of 429-97-9 and won eight state championships in a career that spanned five schools and ended with his retirement in 2011. He had a forty-two game winning streak followed by a fifty-seven game streak. Most of his wins – and all his championships – occurred at Celina and Pilot Point, two small North Texas towns separated by only twelve miles.

Football fans in both towns revere Moore. Some say – only half-jokingly – that his initials stand for "God Almighty." A former Celina school board president who played for Moore calls him simply "The Legend." Supporters still hope that he'll come out of retirement to restore their team to greatness.

How did Moore win so many games decade after decade and become so beloved in the process? He had a system – "The Program," he called it – that he instituted in the early 1960s and gradually perfected. It created lofty expectations for his players both on and off the field and encouraged undying support from the community.

The coach had a keen understanding of football strategy and human nature. He grounded his players in the fundamentals of the sport and made sure they executed with precision and consistency. To motivate his players, Moore used both harsh criticism, occasionally yelling into their facemasks, and quiet support, gently putting his arm around their shoulders.

Moore's intensity was legendary. During halftime of one game, he blistered his team for not hitting hard enough. To drive home his point, he started punching himself in the face, harder and harder, until he broke his glasses and bloodied his face. "See, it don't hurt to hit!" he yelled.

Moore at Aubrey High School, his last coaching stop, 2010.
Photo courtesy of *Denton Record-Chronicle*

Another time, Moore grabbed a soda can and smashed it against his forehead. After a rare loss, Moore would stay up all night, second-guessing his decisions, pacing the floor, and sometimes getting sick to his stomach.

Yet Moore was not a one-dimensional, win-at-all-costs coach. He maintained a quiet, steady demeanor most of the time. Even when he got angry with players, he never belittled them or used profanity. A devout Baptist, he taught Sunday school and served as a church deacon. He had no use for four-letter words, and he made sure his players didn't either.

He found the perfect blend of toughness and tenderness, and his players responded with die-hard devotion. Many ex-players say they never wanted to disappoint Coach Moore – the same way a child never wants to disappoint a parent. Moore keeps stacks of letters that former players have written him over the years. In one, a player apologizes for an off-the-field incident. It must have been bad because he doesn't mention it.

"Dear Coach Moore," the letter begins, "I am truly sorry for my poor decision making last Sunday. I have let you and my teammates down and have done so for the last time. I will start to make the right decisions, and starting Monday I am going to work my hardest to make myself better and totally dedicate myself to the Celina football program."

Another player wrote Moore a letter at the end of an unsuccessful season – that is, one in which the team didn't win the state championship. "I want to apologize for this year's football team. It still hurts me and makes me mad just to think about it. I'm sorry we made you look bad. You know and I know we should be wearing state championship rings right now. Thank you for being such a great role model. I hope someday to become as great a man as you are."

Moore often invited players to his home. He broke down the barrier that normally exists between coaches and athletes. He showed the players his world – his expansive ranch with its horses and cattle – and displayed keen interest in their world. If a kid had a problem at home, Moore wanted to hear about it. Chances are he already knew the family. Moore grew up in a rural area between

Celina and Pilot Point and starred as a running back for Pilot Point High School. He put down roots in the area long before he became a successful coach. His knowledge of the area and its people gave him credibility in the eyes of locals.

Parents trusted Moore and backed his high standards on the field and in the classroom. They didn't mind if he gave their son licks for missing practice, busting curfew, or mouthing off to a teacher. Hell, Moore had likely coached the kid's dad and given him licks too. Many parents viewed him like a trusted relative helping to raise their sons.

Just as kids wanted to please Moore by playing hard, adults wanted to please him by tirelessly backing the football program. Some of the most fervent fans didn't even have a son on the team. In both Celina and Pilot Point, Moore generated so much excitement about football that people with no apparent reason to care about the team cared deeply.

Many joined the Quarterback Club, which met at 5:30 a.m. every Thursday during football season to hear Moore discuss the upcoming opponent. Every year the club raised thousands to buy workout equipment and fund improvements to the stadium. Men volunteered in the adopt-a-player program, serving as a mentor on any issue, football-related or not. Women faithfully decorated the locker room each week and baked goodies for players and coaches.

Football players during Moore's tenure had a support system that most students couldn't imagine. They understood the town's commitment to them – and their obligation to repay it with all-out play. Moore's success had little to do with coaching Xs and Os. It had much more to do with motivating impressionable kids, and impressionable adults, to pull together toward a common goal.

Moore never hid from fans, win or lose. Most mornings he showed up at a popular café in Celina or Pilot Point to mingle with supporters. He welcomed any comment, any critique. Why did he call a certain play? He'd tell them. Why was he starting Smith over Jones? He'd tell them. Moore invited townspeople to practice and welcomed them into the locker room following games. After all, it was *their* team.

Moore rarely had great athletes even on his championship teams. Celina and Pilot Point were small high schools, maybe a couple hundred students, and the talent was sketchy. Some years, Moore had only two or three players who weighed more than two hundred pounds. He never ran a football factory that churned out college prospects. Instead, Moore took slow, skinny kids and coaxed every ounce of talent out of them. He conditioned them superbly and made sure they played almost flawless football. Turnovers, penalties, blown assignments – Moore hated them all. He created intense competition for starting positions even if the two contenders didn't look as if they could play a lick.

Moore's career spanned five decades, and he witnessed great societal change. He began coaching in the early 1960s during the civil rights era and led Pilot Point in 1965 when the school integrated. In some towns around the country, desegregation splintered campuses and athletic teams. Not in Pilot Point. Moore welcomed six black players onto his twenty-four man squad in 1965, and the number of blacks grew every year after that. Moore made clear he wouldn't tolerate racial tension. In the early 1970s, when Moore coached in Celina, he started a string of black quarterbacks, unusual at the time. If blacks labored under the stereotype that they didn't have the composure or leadership skills to play the game's highest-profile position, Moore exploded that myth. His first state championship team in 1974 was quarterbacked by Frank Andrews, an African-American.

Moore had so much success, especially later in his career, that families would move to Celina or Pilot Point so their son could play for him. Opposing coaches accused Moore of recruiting and routinely turned him into the state's athletic governing body. Occasionally it launched investigations but never uncovered any proof of recruiting. Moore vehemently denies that he ever offered inducements to attract players. All he did, he says, was build the finest football program in the region. If families wanted to be part of it, he wouldn't turn them away.

Although Moore won more high school football games than any coach in Texas history, he could have easily won more – if he had just stayed put. Moore jumped between Celina and Pilot Point throughout his career. He had three stints in Pilot Point (1963-1970, 1977-1985, and 2002-2004) and two in Celina (1972-1976 and 1988-2001). Each time he moved, he left behind a top-notch program to face the challenge of rebuilding. He was swayed by friends in both towns who courted him to return, as well as a belief that God was calling him back to the other town.

Winning never was Moore's only goal. Sure, he wanted to nab the state championship every year, but he also wanted to build character in young men and pride in the community. Moore has always prayed daily. When he felt led back to Celina or Pilot Point, he'd pack up and exchange one coach's outfit for another. Even Moore's best friends were mystified by his moves. Moore didn't explain. "I care more about what God thinks than people think."

Moore's last move proved the most divisive. After leading Celina to four straight championships from 1998-2001, he bolted for Pilot Point one final time. In his first year back in Pilot Point, he won his 397th game to surpass the legendary Gordon Wood as Texas' all-time winningest football coach. Meanwhile, Celina failed to win a fifth consecutive title without him. Some people still blame Moore, although the hard feelings have eased over the past decade or so. He now occasionally attends Celina games.

Whenever he's at a game, whether in Celina or Pilot Point, Moore is treated like royalty – although he doesn't ask for special treatment. He'll show up by himself or with his wife of fifty-five years, Lois Ann, and quietly buy a ticket like anyone else. As soon as he enters the stadium, he's mobbed by former players, parents, and childhood friends. Moore's presence brings back fond memories for people in Celina, Pilot Point, and throughout North Texas.

People admire him because he was a winner who taught others how to win – in football and in life. Many former players credit Moore's high standards for their successful careers, stable families, and faith in God. He embraced his platform as a role model to produce good football players and good people.

Each year Moore gave his players a thick playbook. It covered not only the formations they would run but also what they could expect from coaches. The first promise: "To treat you as a man and to love and respect you!" Moore routinely told players he loved them. He could be intense, even intimidating, but he knew when to push and when to let up. Sometimes he'd stop practice and tell his players to take a knee and tell jokes. Or he'd take everyone swimming. The coach managed to make football fun while pushing players to achieve their best.

Today many former players stay in close contact with Moore. They drop by his ranch and offer to do chores for him. Moore has undergone three back surgeries and can't work as hard as he once did. Still, he lifts weights in his garage almost every day to stay in shape. Moore stands five feet and eleven inches and weighs 170 pounds – straight and lean as a 2-by-4. His face is lined and weathered from countless hours on the football field and in the pasture. His ready smile is a little crooked, thanks to a broken cheekbone he got from playing high school football without a facemask. His favorite outfit: Wrangler jeans, boots, and a cowboy hat.

Moore speaks with a slow drawl, often punctuating his sentences with "yes sir" or "no sir." He'd rather hear about someone else's life than talk about his own. When prodded, he can carry on about his players and teams for hours. He has a distinctive vocabulary. A talented player is "a good 'un." A team that won big "beat the dog" out of the opponent. If he wants to express general dismay, he'll say "golly bum." When he's really mad, he might utter "dadgummit." Occasionally, he lets "crap" slip out.

He never had any hobbies. He didn't golf, hunt, or fish. He coached football and tended to the ranch. Vacations? Only if you consider attending a coaches' school or a Fellowship of Christian Athletes conference on vacation. Moore always lived a pure, simple life. Besides football, his greatest loves are his family, his friends, and his church. When he coached, he never earned more than $75,000 a year. His wife and four kids took odd jobs such as cleaning their church and running a dry cleaners to make ends meet.

Moore considered coaching his calling. Early in his career, he thought God was leading him into the ministry, so he abruptly quit coaching and took a principal's job, with plans to attend seminary. He missed coaching, and others persuaded him that his true ministry was on the football field, not in the pulpit. Shortly after he returned to coaching, he won his first of eight state championships, and he started building relationships with players, parents, and townspeople – relationships that have multiplied and deepened over the years.

Who is G.A. Moore? The all-time winningest Texas High School football coach – and so much more.

In His Own Words...Xs and Os

Mistakes Kill You

If you make mistakes, you're going to get beat. I always had trouble with coaches who run around patting kids on the back and saying, "That's all right. That's all right." It ain't all right to make mistakes. It's never been all right to make mistakes. It's not OK to fumble. It's not OK to throw an interception. I don't care if the ball bounces up in the air, and they get it. It's not OK. If we're running plays, and one of them screws up, we're going to talk to them and go over what they did wrong. We stop the play right there in practice. We say, "If you're going to play, you're going to do it right. So get your tail in there and do it right."

Control the Clock, Control the Score

I like good old hard-nosed physical football where we control the clock. We run the ball 70-80 times, the other team runs it about twenty. That's the way I like to play. I'm talking about driving the ball and keeping the ball. I always thought one of the best defenses was a good offense. If we keep the ball, they're not going to score. That's how we won. The first time we get the ball, we like to line up and run right at people and whip them. Let's see if you can stop us. If we can take the opening drive and go down and score, that's going to make a statement for the whole ballgame.

That First Hit

In football, your first few licks are so important. Whoever gets in the first lick is in a whole lot better shape. A lot of kids playing football have some doubts as to how good they are. They have some doubts about the guy playing against them. The first impression you make on that guy is going to be the one he'll remember the rest of that ball-game. Knock the fire out of him on that first play.

Morning Workouts

We had a weight program that started at six o'clock in the morning. We did that for years and years and years. One reason was just to make them pay a price. Another reason was to get them to eat breakfast. Kids won't eat breakfast if you don't make them get up. The big thing about working out in the morning is eating breakfast.

Lifting weights is great, but if you get them out of that bed and make them eat breakfast, they're going to be a healthier kid. If you let them, they'll sleep till 7:30 a.m., then jump up, put their clothes on, and go to class, and they won't eat. It's a habit. Everything is a habit in athletics. You can get in good habits or you can get in bad habits.

Defense is Key

We played defense first everywhere I've ever been. You win with defense. I don't care what level it is. I always told the kids, "If we can get the ball, we can figure out a way to score." I always thought we could score on anybody. Defense is about ninety percent desire and ten percent ability.

Wide Open

Whatever you do, do it wide open. You practice wide open so you'll play wide open. The average play takes only seven seconds. You've got to sell them on the idea that you can go wide open for seven seconds, time after time after time. If we make a mistake, we want to make it going wide open. We can overcome those. People who hesitate get beat.

You don't get hurt when you're playing wide open – most of the time. If you get way ahead of somebody by forty points and they start taking it easy, that's when they're going to get hurt. That's why I always wanted to play those second- and third-string kids when we had a big lead because they're going to play hard, and they're not going to get hurt.

Dictate the Game

Don't ever play to the level of your opponent. Show them how the game is going to be played. If you're a lot better than them, you ought to be ahead 50-0 at half.

Working the Officials

The first thing you do if you're an athlete or a coach is adjust to the officiating. We taught our kids if they're going to let you hold, hold. If they're going to let you jam those guys, jam them. If I can talk an official into something, I'm going to talk him into it. I knew most of them, and I knew pretty well who I could talk to and who I couldn't. Some of them you could say, "Hey, they're holding my defensive end. I want you to watch it." And he's not going to call nothing. Another guy you could say the same thing to, and he'll call it the next time.

The 400 Yard Run

One thing I've always done is make our kids run the 400 because I knew how much it hurts to run that thing. We've been doing that for years and years. I can run kids in 400s and tell you a whole lot about them because it's going to hurt, and you're going to see how they react when the pain hits and they still have to finish. I loved running 400s because I felt like you had to have something to hang your hat on that gives your team an advantage. And running 400s is one of those things. If you played for us, you ran a 400. The quarterbacks always ran against each other. If they didn't put out and suck up their guts and run, they weren't going to play quarterback. I don't want anybody standing in front of the huddle that can't run a 400. It makes an impression on those guys that are watching.

Chapter 2
<u>A Rookie Coach Builds a Team</u>

Only six players showed up.

G.A. Moore, the new football coach at tiny Bryson High School, looked at his meager squad on the weed-choked practice field and sighed. He'd sent letters to every boy in school – all two dozen – and urged them to come out for the first practice on a Monday morning in mid-August 1962. This practice was the beginning of a record-setting career for Moore, but he didn't even have enough players to field a team.

"Well," the twenty-three year old, flat-topped Moore told his players, "let's get to work."

The boys, wearing hand-me-down shoulder pads and helmets, ran drills and learned plays under the critical but encouraging eye of Coach Moore. With a whistle draped around his neck, he ran the practice alone. The poor district in the north central Texas town of only 545 couldn't afford an assistant coach.

After two hours in the searing sun, the boys hoped they were finished with practice. But they weren't. Moore told them to climb into his car – a cavernous and creaky 1951 Ford Crown Victoria. "We're going to find some more players," the coach announced. The boys, who had just met their new coach, didn't protest. Moore turned to the three seniors – Jimmy Beatty, Craig Stamper and George Tuel – and asked for directions to the homes of boys who didn't show up for practice. They guided him down dusty gravel roads to one boy's house, then another, and another.

At each stop, the trio got out of the car and walked with Moore to the door. They introduced the new coach to the prospective player's father. Moore shook hands firmly and said he'd sure like his son to come out for football.

High school football wasn't a huge deal in Bryson. The town was founded in the late 1870s but didn't begin to grow until oil was discovered and the railroad reached its border in 1903. By the mid-1940s, the town reached its peak population of 806 – the second-largest town in Jack County. In subsequent decades, oil production dipped, and so did the population. When Moore arrived as coach in 1962, the town didn't have a single traffic light.

At that point, the Bryson Cowboys hadn't won a game in more than two seasons. Unlike many small Texas towns, the people of Bryson didn't flock to the brightly lit stadium on Friday nights as if they were headed to church. Moore had to build not only a winning football team but a fan base. He was up for the challenge.

"We're going to win," he promised the dads on their doorsteps.

His sales pitch worked. Moore enlisted seven more players on that two-hour impromptu recruiting trip, bringing the squad to thirteen. That would be enough. Bryson High School was so small that it played eight-man football instead of the traditional eleven-man. Moore didn't waste any time with his new recruits. He told them to meet at the practice field right then, and they did. The coach turned the Crown Victoria back toward the high school and led the way.

What did the players think of their new coach? "Well, he wasn't much older than us," recalls Tuel, the quarterback. "But he was real likeable. He was a good coach."

Moore had an intensity they hadn't seen in previous coaches. He insisted they run drills and plays over and over until they eliminated mistakes. If he didn't think the players were hitting hard enough, he'd run to the field house and put on some pads himself. He dared the players to hit him as hard as they could – all in an effort to make them tougher. "It wasn't very often that you got to take a shot at a coach," says Stamper, a stocky tackle. Pete Pippen, another tackle, recalls, "He'd pop some leather with you. He wasn't a real big man, but he could hold his own."

The Cowboys had only three weeks to prepare for their first game. They were going on the road to play the mighty Prosper Eagles, a team that had humiliated Bryson 76-0 the previous year. Outwardly Moore projected confidence to his players, but inwardly, he feared his small and slow players were headed for a whipping. He needed any edge he could get. So he decided to take his players to his parents' house outside Pilot Point for a pregame meal.

When Moore starred as a running back for the Pilot Point Bearcats, his momma always fixed him a meal of vegetable soup, cheese toast, and sweet tea before every game. The meal, and a little nap afterward, always seemed to get him primed for kickoff. Why wouldn't the same ritual work for the Bryson team?

Moore's parents, Gary and Nell Moore, gladly opened their home to the squad. The bus ride from Bryson to the Moore place took almost two hours. When the boys finished their meal, Coach Moore had them lie down on the living room floor and dimmed the lights. Just as he'd done as a player, Moore wanted his players to rest and focus on the game ahead.

"We stayed right there until time for the ballgame," Moore recalls.

After two hours, he rousted the boys and loaded them back on the school bus. The Prosper stadium was only twenty minutes away. On the way, Moore could see that his players would face another obstacle besides the talented Prosper team: the weather. "It came a flood, a monsoon," Moore says. One end zone was completely under water. On the sidelines, Moore and the players stood in ankle-deep water. "Nobody would play in that kind of weather today." Despite the dismal conditions and a fearsome opponent, the Cowboys were eager to get started. "I was excited," Moore says, "and the kids were excited."

The driving rain prevented either team from passing the ball effectively. The coaches called run after run, hoping to move the ball through the muck into the end zone. In a game with several fumbles, Prosper coughed up the ball first. Bryson recovered, and Tuel fed the ball repeatedly to Beatty, a burly, straight-ahead runner. His powerful style suited the sloppy conditions that rendered Prosper's speed advantage useless. "The mud and rain helped us," Tuel says. "You'd get tackled and get a face full of water. It was hard to hold onto the ball, as wet as it was."

Shortly before halftime, Beatty plowed into the end zone to give Bryson a 6-0 lead. The extra point attempt failed, but it didn't matter. Moore's aggressive, blitzing defense, which would become his trademark, kept Prosper off guard and out of the end zone. The slim lead held up in the second half, and Bryson scored an unlikely, inspirational victory that launched Moore's career and turned around Bryson's football fortunes.

Afterward the bitter Prosper players didn't linger to congratulate the Bryson squad. They quickly boarded their bus. "They couldn't believe we whipped their butts," says Stamper, smiling. Says James Ranspot, another player, "*Nobody* in Prosper could believe it."

Moore credits his team's preparation and the goopy field for the win. "The rain was such an equalizer," he says. "They thought it wasn't going to be a ballgame." But he also gives credit to a higher source: God. Moore's Christian faith had always been a guiding force in his life, and he thought the Lord orchestrated his first win. "I should have known right then that the Good Lord had a hand in what was taking place in my life because we had no business even being on the field with those people."

After the game, Moore hopped onto the bus and delivered his first postgame victory speech. "I told them it didn't make any difference what happened next. I would never forget this game. You'd have thought we'd won the state championship. We were so happy. Those guys went out there and did something nobody would have given them any chance of doing. That's one of the great things about football, and I got a taste of it the first game I ever got to coach."

The driving rain still hadn't stopped when the game ended. So Moore told the bus driver to head to the nearby town of Denton and wait out the storm. They stopped at a Humble station, and Moore bought his mud-drenched players Cokes and candy bars. Their joyful shouts echoed throughout the bus.

Before long, other Bryson celebrants arrived. Cars containing cheerleaders, parents of players, and a few die-hard fans pulled up next to the bus. They welcomed the victory like a farmer welcomes rain during a drought. The grinning, fresh-faced rookie coach was uniting and lifting up a bedraggled community. "Those people who were there were so excited," Moore says. "We had a party until about 4:30 or 5:00 in the morning. The water finally went down, and we were able to go back to Bryson. That was such a thrill to be a part of."

Moore never expected to start his coaching career in Bryson. He got the job only weeks before the start of the 1962 season because of Barrett Reeves, his former Pilot Point coach. Reeves had coached at Bryson before taking over the Pilot Point program when Moore was a sophomore.

Reeves had been the last winning coach in Bryson, and he was still a beloved figure. When he heard about the Bryson opening, he called Moore and encouraged him to apply. Moore and Reeves drove to Bryson to meet the superintendent. That night, the school board met and voted unanimously to hire Moore. "They hired me because of Barrett Reeves, really. He was a big hero out there. It had been six or seven years since he was out there, and they hadn't won."

Moore with his wife, Lois Ann, at Celina stadium, 2015.
Photo courtesy of Phil Bailiff

Ironically Moore had never watched an eight-man football game before he was hired. He hadn't given any thought to how he would adjust his plays to the smaller team size.

"I just wanted to coach. I was ready to do anything. I was in hog heaven."

***

When G.A. Moore moved to Bryson, he took his new wife, Lois Ann. He credits much of his coaching success over the years to her. She never complained when he watched game film hour after hour, night after night. She came to every game and rejoiced over every victory and agonized over every defeat – just like G.A. After they had kids, Lois Ann often did the bulk of the parenting so G.A. could focus on coaching.

G.A. and Lois Ann married in May 1961 in Pilot Point and had their first child, Pam, in 1962. They would have three more. He borrowed his dad's cattle trailer and loaded it full of used furniture from a thrift store to make the move to Bryson. He and Lois Ann settled into a barebones government-subsidized housing complex a few blocks from the high school. The rent was twenty-five dollars a month. "We didn't have *nothing*," Moore recalls.

Still he and Lois Ann made fond memories in Bryson. They met several other teachers who lived in the red-brick, barrack-style apartments, and they made more friends at First Baptist Church around the corner. They cherished their time with newborn Pam. "She was a little bitty rascal," the coach says.

He and Lois Ann had started dating when he was a freshman football player at North Texas State University and she was a high school sophomore in Pilot Point. One of Moore's friends, Bobby Richardson, wanted to go out with a girl he knew. Moore approached the girl, but the only way she would go out with Bobby was on a double date.

"Why don't you go with us?" she asked G.A. "You can go with Lois Ann Graves."

"Well," he replied, "OK."

He remembered Lois Ann from high school, but only vaguely. After all, he was a senior, and she was only a freshman. Still he was excited about the date, and he knew his friend would be glad he'd brokered the deal. On the date, the four of them drove to Dairy Queen for drinks and then walked around the Pilot Point square. Moore doesn't remember the details of the outing as much as he does his impression of Lois Ann.

"She was the funniest, silliest girl I'd ever been around in my life," Moore says. "She was just different. I had more fun with her than any other girl I had ever dated."

At the end of the evening, G.A. took Lois Ann home, and he drove back to his college dorm a half-hour away in Denton. He still dated college women, but his heart was set on Lois Ann. Gradually they spent more time together and soon were dating exclusively. Two years later, as soon as she graduated from high school, they planned to marry. They picked a date and put an announcement in the newspaper. Then a problem arose. G.A. was a Baptist, and Lois Ann went to the Assembly of God church. He had always assumed Lois Ann would join him as a Baptist, but her mother protested. She had raised Lois Ann in the Assembly of God church, and she wanted her daughter to keep going there after her marriage.

G.A. dug in his heels. He wasn't about to turn his back on his Baptist roots. He had attended the Assembly of God a time or two and didn't like the charismatic worship style. "I thought the Baptist church was the only church. My parents taught me that a family needed to go to church together, and I told Lois Ann we needed to go to the same church."

As hard as he tried to persuade Lois Ann, she wouldn't go against her mother's wishes. "So we split up," Moore says. "We broke our engagement." He demanded the engagement ring back and sold it to a friend. "I think I gave two hundred dollars for it and sold it for one hundred dollars."

For two weeks, G.A. and Lois Ann didn't talk. "I was mad at her and mad at her momma." Slowly, however, the chill between them thawed, and they resumed dating. A year after their original wedding date, in May 1961, G.A. and Lois Ann married. Looking back, G.A. admits he was too stubborn in his refusal to attend the Assembly of God church. "I was hard-headed – that's all it was. I know it, dang it."

As a concession to her mother, Lois Ann attended the Baptist church with G.A. but didn't join for two years. Once she made the decision, though, Lois Ann became active in the church. "There are many things I am proud of about my wife, and one is she has been a worker in the church ever since then." Her mother later accepted Lois Ann's decision to become a Baptist, and G.A. made peace with his mother-in-law. "Her mom and I eventually got along great."

In Bryson, G.A. and Lois strengthened their young marriage. As newlyweds, they needed time away from their parents to build their own identity as a couple. "Lois Ann is the greatest thing that's ever happened to me. She loves football. I don't know how many people have told me she's the perfect coach's wife. I never had any problems at home. A lot of coaches do."

***

When Moore started college, he never imagined being a coach. Instead he wanted to be a professional football player, and that dream seemed within reach given his talent. Moore earned a football scholarship to North Texas State University in1957 after a standout career as a defensive back and running back at Pilot Point High School. He rushed for more than two thousand yards, scored more than twenty touchdowns, and earned All-State honors.

Moore wasn't big – only five feet and eleven inches and 170 pounds, but he was blazing fast, setting the school record for the one hundred yard dash at 10.2 seconds. When he arrived at North Texas as a freshman, he was full of confidence. "I hate to say it now, but I was probably a little too cocky. I thought I could do things I probably couldn't."

Back then, freshmen couldn't play on the varsity team. But they practiced with the varsity, and Moore's eyes were opened when he encountered a star running back named Abner Haynes. He was one of the few black players at North Texas, which had recently integrated. Haynes, a year older than Moore, was bigger, faster, and shiftier – and he played the same position. After Haynes left North Texas, he starred in the upstart American Football League, winning Most Valuable Player and Rookie of the Year honors in 1960. In practice, Moore's assignment was to defend Haynes – or at least to try.

"I never will forget playing against him. I found out Abner could do some of the things I wished I could do. I remember one time, we were scrimmaging the varsity, and Abner runs an end sweep. He comes around right against the sideline, and I'm coming across the field, thinking to myself, *I'm fixing to lay him out. I'm fixing to show him something.* I ducked my head and just sailed through the air. I landed out of bounds and looked up. He was going on down the sidelines, scoring. I didn't even touch him. That was my introduction to what a real running back could do."

By Moore's sophomore year, he hoped to earn some playing time in the backfield, relieving Haynes. After a strong showing in spring training, Moore thought he was making a name for himself. Early in the season, however, he suffered a broken wrist in practice. He took a handoff and broke the line of scrimmage when a linebacker rammed his helmet directly into Moore's left wrist. It snapped. "I finished scrimmage, but it swelled up at night. The doc X-rayed it and said it was broke."

Moore in his college football days as a sophomore, 1958

Doctors placed a cast on his wrist and told him his season was finished. In the spring, Moore hoped to resume practice and prepare for his junior year, but doctors said the wrist still needed more time to heal. He wore a cast over the summer, getting it off in time for fall practice. During two-a-day workouts, the weak wrist snapped again. This time, there wouldn't be another comeback. Moore's college career ended before it could blossom. He sank into depression. "I thought my life was over. Up until that point, football had been my life."

Distraught, Moore dropped out of college and moved back home. He went to work on a quarter horse ranch. "I didn't handle it very well. I was upset and just ready to quit school and change direction." A teammate, Charlie Cole, remembers how the injury devastated Moore. "He really got down. He probably went into a slight depression. G.A. had all kinds of potential."

During his semester away from college, however, Moore came to terms with his injury. He re-enrolled at North Texas in spring 1960, intent on getting an education. Before his injury, he was a half-hearted student, achieving just enough academically to remain eligible for football. "I woke up when I couldn't play football anymore and decided I wanted to get an education. I started studying, and I started making good grades. It's amazing what happens when you study."

Focused on academics, Moore graduated on time in 1962. Looking back, he says he's now thankful for the wrist injury. It led him into coaching instead of chasing what he admits was an unrealistic dream of playing pro ball. The broken wrist might also have saved him from more serious injury. Moore played mostly defense in college. And he played like a kamikaze pilot, crashing his body into opposing players without regard for his own safety. He suffered several concussions, broken ribs, and a fractured collarbone.

"I got knocked out two or three times. I was stupid, I guess. I remember getting hit one time, and everything went black. I could get up on one knee, but I couldn't see a lick. Back then, if you didn't go to the wrong huddle and you could count how many fingers somebody was holding up, they'd send you back in. It was kind of a game we played – we'd try to hit somebody so hard that they'd go out of the game. Nobody thought it was dirty; that was just football. I'd probably have gotten killed if I'd kept on playing."

In one practice drill at the time, coaches lined up two players ten yards apart and made them run full speed into each other, heads down like battering rams. "It wasn't very smart. I'd probably have broken my neck because I really liked to hit. I feel like the Lord took care of me." Teammate Dan Smith remembers Moore's aggressiveness as a player. He also recalls Moore's understanding of football strategy – a characteristic that would make him an outstanding coach. "He knew the game. He knew what to do and when to do it. I don't remember him talking about coaching, but it was pretty evident he had the ability to do so."

Smith followed Moore's career and admired his success. "It wasn't just his coaching ability. It was his ability to relate to young people. He knows how to help young people grow up and be men. He's influenced more people than anybody would ever know. I've seen him take a bunch of small, iffy kids that were outmanned and end up on top at the end of the game because they knew what to do. He could always get more out of a kid than anybody I've ever seen – bar none. The players had faith in him. They knew if he they did what he told them, they would be successful. He was able to pull out of those kids what they didn't know they had."

***

During his time at North Texas, Moore learned about racism. When the team traveled, some restaurants wouldn't serve Haynes and the few other black players. Some motels wouldn't let them stay there. Often the entire team refused to go to a restaurant or motel if it didn't welcome the black players, Moore says. "We stayed a lot of times in second-rate hotels because we had blacks. We all stayed where he [Haynes] stayed."

Moore attended segregated schools in Pilot Point, but he had black friends whose families also farmed. Blacks were welcome in his parents' home anytime, he says. "At a lot of cafes, blacks had to eat in the back. At some houses, people would make blacks eat out in the yard. My mother and dad were different. Everybody ate at the table with us. That's just the way I was raised."

Moore didn't have any black players at Bryson, but he did at every other coaching stop in his career. In 1965, when he was coaching at his alma mater Pilot Point, the school integrated. Moore immediately welcomed several blacks onto the team, and they competed for starting positions. In the early and mid-1970s when Moore was coaching at Celina, he started a succession of black quarterbacks. At the time, many white coaches played blacks at every position – except quarterback, the spot that required the most leadership and afforded the highest profile. Frank Andrews played quarterback for Celina from 1972 to 1974. He doesn't recall any racial tension on the team or any whites questioning why he should be allowed to play quarterback.

"I never had any problems," Andrews says. "If anybody said anything, I didn't hear about it. We won quite a few games, so I didn't get a lot of pressure. Coach Moore was a very good coach. We learned quite a bit from him as a football team."

***

In 1962, after the exhilaration of Bryson's 6-0 opening game victory, disappointment followed. In the second game, the Cowboys were manhandled by Gunter 36-6. There would be no Cinderella story sequel.

In the third game, Bryson regrouped and hammered Bellevue 50-12. With the fourth game approaching, Bryson faced a challenging foe: Pilot Point. The Cowboys would be playing the Pilot Point junior varsity, which played eleven-man football. Bryson, because of its smaller size, played eight-man. For the first time all season, Moore had to design a game plan with extra players on each side of the ball. To flesh out his meager roster, the coach added two players for the Pilot Point game. Neither he nor his players knew if they could compete with a school with such a proud football heritage.

After the opening kickoff, Bryson scored first. Then again – and again, and again. Final score: Bryson 50, Pilot Point 0. The celebration rivaled the one from three weeks earlier when Bryson somehow beat Prosper. Moore had given his squad a fiery pep talk before the Pilot Point game, and it paid off. "He wanted to win that game more than any of them," Tuel says.

After the game, a couple of Moore's old friends from Pilot Point called and said he should come back home and coach the Bearcats. He laughed off their offer. He still had work to do in Bryson.

The next two weeks, Bryson suffered blowout losses: 58-22 to Goree and 38-6 to Harrold. After six games, the Cowboys stood at 3-3. A win in week seven pushed the record to 4-3. Then Bryson endured a humiliating defeat – 68-10 to Oklaunion. It would be the worst loss of this season – or any season in Moore's legendary career. Ironically, Bryson took an early 10-0 lead against Oklaunion. He called some reverses and other trick plays – "junk," he says. Then the superior Oklaunion squad woke from its slumber and scored sixty-eight unanswered points.

"We made them mad," Moore says. "Then we couldn't stay on the field with those people. Lord of mercy, they were in a different league. They had two big old boys who weighed two hundred and something pounds. I can still remember them. We didn't have anybody on our team who could tackle them suckers. They tore us up. That was an education."

Bryson rebounded the next week, scoring a solid 24-14 win over Windthorst to move to 5-4. In the final game of the year, Bryson played without two of its best players, quarterback Tuel and running back Beatty, who were both injured. The Cowboys lost to Woodson, 38-30, to finish the season at 5-5.

Still, the record was a huge improvement from 0-10 the previous year. "We beat a bunch of teams we weren't supposed to beat," Tuel says. Moore had made the players believe in themselves – and made townspeople excited about Bryson football again. "It was quite an experience that year. Those kids got where they weren't scared of anybody. We worked hard, and everybody played. Boy, we had a good time. I loved those kids."

The players liked their new coach, but they quickly learned that he was demanding. He wouldn't accept anything less than one hundred percent effort all the time. Pippen remembers that Moore yanked him out of a game one time.

"He said, 'Pippen, do you want to play ball tonight or do you want to sit on the bench?' I said, 'I thought I was playing ball.' He said, 'No, you're not giving half of what you should give.' He grabbed me by the back of the neck and kicked me in the hiney. I said, 'If you let me go back in, I guarantee you I'll play a ballgame.' And he did."

Moore stayed busy the entire year. Not only did he coach the football team by himself and mow the practice field, but he also coached the boys' and girls' basketball and track teams. He taught a full load of classes. "Shoot, I coached everything. If they had it, I coached it." Did he resent being overworked? Not at all. "After growing up working ten hours a day in the cotton fields, this wasn't like work. It was fun."

Moore was overworked and underpaid. His salary was only $4,750. He was promised a five hundred dollar raise if he stayed for a second season. He considered it but was growing homesick. "Lois Ann and I went home to Pilot Point nearly every weekend after the football season was over. I was close to my family, and I'd never been away from home that much."

He put out some feelers and was offered the head football job in Callisburg, thirty miles north of Pilot Point. Then the Pilot Point job came open, and he jumped at the chance to return to his alma mater. Moore cured his homesickness and set himself on a path toward multiple state championships and hundreds of victories. "We hated to see him leave, but we weren't surprised," Ranspot says. "Most of the coaches who came to Bryson didn't even unpack their suitcases."

"I had a lot of fun at Bryson. I've got some great memories, but the only place I wanted to coach was Pilot Point. I always wanted Pilot Point to be the best. That's the main reason I came back," says Moore.

In His Own Words...Motivation

<u>Always the Underdog</u>

I played every game like we were the underdog. I don't care if we were favored by thirty points, we're going to prepare a game plan like we're the underdog. Usually, we practiced what we called junk plays after practice for fifteen or thirty minutes – reverse passes and throwbacks. We had a last-second play we worked on a lot – a hook-and-ladder. If you're the underdog, you'd better have some junk.

<u>Mental Toughness</u>

Everyone wants to win when the game starts. It's who wants to win in the last quarter that counts. When two teams are competing, what you're watching is more a contest of wills than of skills. The stronger will usually overcomes skill. We want to play football at a level that is very difficult for our opponents to maintain for forty-eight minutes. Force the opponent to play full speed every play, knowing that when the game is on the line in the fourth quarter, there is a high probability that fatigue will destroy his will. If we are close going into the fourth quarter, the advantage is ours.

<u>Talent is Secondary</u>

The teams with the best athletes very seldom win state championships. You can take a bunch of kids that have a great attitude and bond together and really want to be a team, and they can win a championship. They get on a roll, and they're all sacrificing. So many of the big school coaches have the mentality, "If I've got athletes better than you, I'm going to win. If you have the best athletes, you're going to win." That's not right.

Lois Ann [my wife] could coach teams with better athletes. I want to beat people we don't have any business beating. We approached every game as if we were the underdog. I don't care who we're playing. So many years, we weren't bigger, so we had to be faster and stronger. We spent a lot of time in the weight room and a lot of time on agility drills and quickness drills. We'd tumble, turn flips, and run the ropes. I always had a theory that we're going to outwork everybody we play, period. We're going to outwork them in the offseason. We're going to outwork them in the summer. We're going to outwork them during the season. And that's going to give us an advantage.

The last two years I coached, we played with a 160 pound guard and a 155 pound center. We were playing guys that were six feet, six inches and 275 and were going to Division I schools. It's like David and Goliath. But if we've got the slingshot, we're going to do something. We're going to figure out a way to get around those folks. We're not going to line up and run over them. We run reverse passes and traps. Our quarterbacks did a lot of reading at the line. If you've got a big old defensive tackle who weighs 270, we can hit a dive to the inside of him.

The Best

Be the best you can be. That's pretty simple. Be the best that you can be. Don't accept anything less than the best. Don't accept anything less than the best from your teammate.

Pep Talks

If we're playing somebody that's 0-9, I'm going to worry a whole lot more about that speech than if we're playing somebody that's 9-0. If we're playing somebody who ain't worth a dern, then the kids maybe won't be ready to play. Somebody better be getting on them and getting them straightened out. I usually chewed them out and got mad at them and kicked a trash can or something to try to get their attention.

At halftime, it just depended on how the game was going. I just got up and went to talking. It's a gut feeling, mainly. I never will forget one time we were playing Wichita Falls in the playoffs. We weren't playing good. I told Butch [Ford, an assistant coach], "I'm going to wait a minute before I go in there at halftime. Set that trash can out. When I walk in, I'm going to kick it and get their attention and shake them up." I walked in and kicked that trash can, and it had concrete or something in that sucker. I thought I had broken my foot, and this is halftime of a big playoff game. I was trying to talk to them and, man, my foot was hurting like the dickens. That was funny after it was all over. Butch said, "I was going to try to tell you not to kick that trash can when you came in there. There was something wrong with that thing."

Confidence

Too many folks are not successful because they don't have confidence in themselves. I always thought I could do anything – play football, baseball, basketball, run track, rope calves – better than anybody else. That's what I tried to do. I might have too much confidence in myself. My wife says I do.

Everyone Matters

Everybody on a team is either helping or hurting. I tell the kids that we don't have anybody on the sidelines that is not part of this team. Not everybody will play, but they can have a big influence on the team. They could be the first one on the field to congratulate somebody for making a good block or a good kick. There are no neutral observers. If you are not between the lines, make every effort to be a positive factor for your team.

Momentum

We used to put a lot of emphasis on how we started out the year, winning that first ballgame and impressing everybody. We changed all that. The non-district schedule is just a workout. You want to make sure you have the right people playing at the right place. When you get into district, you move up to another level because you're getting ready for the playoffs. That's all it is – preparation for the playoffs. And when you get in the playoffs, you move up another level.

You have to get everything headed in the right direction at the right time. You do that by working together and having kids that are committed to each other. I want to be a lot better at the end of the year than we are at first. The most important games are the end of the year. If you're a coach, the only way to be really satisfied is to win that last ballgame. That means you won the state championship.

Underachievers

There's kids like that everywhere. Sometimes you can't do anything about it. You can just keep trying and trying, hoping you'll hit that hot button. If you do, those guys will turn.

Chapter 3
<u>Going Home</u>

G. A. Moore still remembers a paper he wrote for his high school English teacher, Miss Savage.

In it, he laid out his goals in life – first to star as a professional football player, then to return to Pilot Point High School and develop a championship football program. "Miss Savage wrote me a note and told me how much she liked what I'd said. She said, 'I want to make sure you strive to do exactly what you're saying.'"

Moore loved football from a young age. He remembers the first football he ever owned. He got it from his Uncle Fred when he was only four years old. "I was a little bitty sucker. I had that ball for years and years. I used to carry it to school every day when I was in grade school." When he got a little older, Moore would watch another relative, Uncle Charles, play football at nearby Celina High School. He was a fast, shifty running back – and his success inspired Moore to dream of carrying the ball and scoring touchdowns. "He was one of my football heroes. He helped me get interested in playing ball."

In those days, Pilot Point was so small that it didn't have youth sports leagues. So Moore and his buddies played pickup football games for hours in the fields. "All we ever wanted to do was play ball." Moore was the fastest, most talented player, but he wouldn't have a chance to showcase his talents to a crowd until he joined the high school team as a freshman. He couldn't wait. His mother, however, didn't share his enthusiasm for football. She was afraid that G.A., who was only five feet, nine inches and 140 pounds, would get hurt. His dad, whom G.A. idolized, intervened. "Daddy took me off and put his arm around me and said, 'Hey, don't worry about it. I'll take care of it.'"

He did. Whatever his dad said to his mom worked. G.A. got to play.

Sophomore Moore (right) with Pilot Point High School teammate, junior Vernon Cole, 1955

Moore (center) as a freshman at Pilot Point. His teammates, left to right: Tucky Dunn, G.B. Walling, Doug Boswell, and Vernon Cole, 1954

In his first game, he intercepted two passes and carried the ball several times on offense. His dad rushed up to him after the game, excitement lighting up his face. "He said, 'I was so proud of you!'" By the third game, Moore had become the starting running back – and a star. "Football wasn't just fun to him," says Tuck Dunn, a childhood friend. "He really wanted to be good – and he was. He gave it all he had. He was a little ahead of most players then."

Moore did well as a freshman, but the team didn't. It finished a disappointing 3-6-1. The next year, Pilot Point got a new coach, Barrett Reeves. Late in Moore's sophomore season, Pilot Point faced its toughest opponent, Lewisville. The Fighting Farmers, as they were called, were undefeated and ranked first in the state. "They'd been beating everybody bad, bad, bad," Moore says. Coach Reeves pulled out all the stops to try to motivate the team and the town. He held daily pep rallies that were packed. Prominent townspeople spoke, encouraging the boys to pull off an upset. Reeves instructed the players to stay home every night and think about the game. "I dreamed every night about that ballgame," Moore says. "The night before the game, I dreamed we won."

When the game began, Moore's dream seemed like pure fantasy. Lewisville ran back the opening kickoff for a touchdown and built a commanding 19-0 halftime lead. In the second half, Pilot Point chipped away at the lead and narrowed the gap to 19-14 with a minute left. Moore then made a play that people still talk about today. He caught a screen pass from quarterback Vernon Cole, who later starred at North Texas State University, and weaved 50 yards for a touchdown to give Pilot Point a 20-19 win. The Bearcats had completed an improbable comeback against a seemingly invincible opponent. "It was so exciting," Moore says. "It was my first great, great experience in football."

The impact of the inspirational win stayed with Moore throughout his playing and coaching career. "That was the first time I realized you don't have to be the best team to win," he says. "If you could just get the right attitude and get everybody pulling together, they could do things they didn't think they could do. We beat a team twice as good as we were, and we did it because we wanted it so bad." After the game, the school opened the gym, and townspeople poured in to celebrate the victory. Later, as a coach, he would recall the impact of the town's fervor on the players. "When we played, we always had more fans than the other team. I learned that you need support from the town. No coach can do things by himself."

The victory over Lewisville served as a springboard for the rest of the season. Pilot Point finished 6-4 to win its first district championship since 1946, but the Bearcats drew a daunting first-round opponent, Paducah. Like Lewisville, Paducah entered the game against Pilot Point undefeated, but this game didn't have a happy ending. Paducah obliterated Pilot Point 70-0. "We got the dog beat out of us," Moore says. "They had a kid named Bibby, a fullback, and he weighed 210 pounds. That game was in 1954, and I can still remember him."

As a junior, Moore continued to improve. He rushed for more than a thousand yards for the first time and scored eighty-four points. In one article, the local newspaper called Moore "a virtual Mr. Touchdown" for his scoring prowess. Pilot Point finished 7-3, slightly better than the year before, but missed the playoffs. When his senior year approached, Moore was brimming with confidence, even cockiness. "I didn't think anybody could touch us, and I didn't think anybody could tackle me." The *Pilot Point Post-Signal* shared his optimism, calling Moore "a slippery, triple-threat, pass-stealing artist who has been the oppositions' headache for the last two years." Another article said simply, "Moore is the finest running back this school has had in years."

The season, however, quickly turned sour. In a scrimmage before the first game, Moore suffered a broken cheekbone. He was carrying the ball when a tackler's knee crashed into his face, knocking him out. An ambulance raced Moore to nearby Denton, then on to Dallas for surgery. Doctors wired his cheekbone back together. To this day, Moore lacks feeling in the right side of his face, and his smile is slightly crooked. He might have avoided the injury if he'd worn a facemask. But in the mid-1950s, facemasks were a new innovation. Pilot Point received its first shipment of facemasks only a day before the scrimmage in which Moore was injured. He decided not to get one. He considered it a badge of honor to play without a facemask.

"From the time football started in the fall until it was over, we never had any skin on our nose. We'd get scabs, and we'd pick them off before the game started. You'd wipe the blood around on your face, just to look mean – to make people think you'd really hit somebody."

Because of the broken cheekbone, Moore missed the first four games of the season. When he returned, he realized the long layoff had affected his conditioning. In a game late in the season, Pilot Point trailed, 18-13, when Moore took a handoff, broke a couple of tackles, and sprinted more than fifty yards for what appeared to be the winning touchdown. An opposing player caught the normally fleet-footed Moore from behind – unheard of – and wrestled him to the ground at the two yard line.

Pilot Point failed in four tries to score. Moore still blames himself for the defeat. "I lost more sleep over that game than any I've ever been associated with. I shouldn't have let that sucker catch me. I should have made sure we won the ballgame, and I didn't get it done. That game still bothers me – years and years and years later. That's how much of an impression football had on me."

***

G.A. Moore grew up poor. He and his two sisters – one older, one younger – lived with their parents on a family farm in the unincorporated community of Mustang, just east of Pilot Point. G.A.'s grandfather and uncles also helped farm the land, which totaled about five hundred acres. It had been in the family since the early 1900s. The Moores had cattle and horses and grew a variety of crops, such as cotton, corn, and wheat. In the summer, G.A. worked ten hours a day in the fields. He and the others started at 7:00 a.m., took off an hour for lunch, and finished at 6:00 p.m. "All the kids out here worked like that," Moore says. The back-breaking labor taught him discipline and the value of working with others to accomplish a goal. It also taught him he didn't want to be a farmer. Coaching would be his escape.

G.A.'s parents, Gary and Nell, dropped out of high school and married when he was eighteen and she was sixteen. Gary immediately joined his father in working the land. Times were so tough, however, that they often took other jobs too. G.A.'s dad, for instance, left home for weeks at a time on occasion. He worked in the oilfield, then at a leather goods factory in Dallas, and for an aircraft manufacturer in Grand Prairie near Dallas. Nell, when she wasn't working in the fields herself, also had a job with a defense contractor, and she cooked in the school cafeteria.

G.A. and his sisters, Margie and Peggy, used to accompany their mom to the lunchroom at 5:00 a.m. If they mopped the floors, they got a free breakfast, which cost everyone else twenty-five cents. "For a long time, we struggled to get by," G.A. recalls. "Both of my parents were hard workers. They worked so hard because our family would starve if they didn't."

G.A. speaks fondly of his parents, but they didn't put up with any nonsense. "Mother and Daddy were pretty strict. They beat the dog out of me all the time." Both had firm ideas of parenting. When his dad found out G.A. had been smoking cigarettes as a young kid, he decided to teach his son a lesson. He bought him a pack of cigarettes – Chesterfields – and sent G.A. to his room. "He told me, 'All right, here's your cigarettes. Now get your little butt in there and go to smoking them.' He made me smoke one right after the other. I got sick. Gosh dang, it liked to kill me. I quit smoking for a while."

Moore, four years old with older sister Peggy, eleven years old, 1942

Later his dad thought it was time for G.A. to learn to swim, so he left town and told him to be swimming by the time he returned. "We had a horse tank. He told me, 'You better know how to swim when I get back, or I'm throwing your little butt in the tank, and you'll have to swim out.' When he got back, I could swim up and down that tank. I didn't want him throwing me in."

Gary Moore may have practiced tough love, but G.A. idolized him. "When I was growing up, my dad was my hero. I thought he could do anything better than anybody in the world. I thought he could ride a horse and rope calves

Moore at age four on his stallion Lucas, 1942

Moore in his front yard when he was in the fifth grade

and drive a car better than anybody else. Being with him was just a great time for me. He was hard on me, but he also taught me to do so many things that I felt other kids didn't have the opportunity to learn because their dad didn't spend time with them. I always tried to pattern my life after him."

G.A. went to church with his parents every Sunday at Mustang Baptist Church, a short walk from their house. In the summers, the church hosted two-week revivals with an out-of-town preacher. Revival services were held at 10:00 a.m. and 7:00 p.m., and G.A. attended every one. By the time he was eight, his parents wanted him to walk down the aisle and accept Jesus as his savior. His mom, who led the singing, was the most insistent. Then his dad started pressuring him too. "We were going to town, and I remember Daddy asked me, 'Hey, you've kind of been under conviction about becoming a Christian, haven't you?' I stuttered and stammered around. I don't know what I said. He told me, 'I think that's something you need to go ahead and get done.' That's all it took."

That evening at the revival service, little G.A. stood up in the pew and walked determinedly down the aisle to meet the evangelist at the front. He knelt in prayer with him. Suddenly he felt a hand on his left shoulder. "My mother had come down and was praying with me. To this day, I remember the warmth and love I felt when I looked over to see my mother kneeling beside me." When G.A. got older, she used to put an open Bible on his pillow every night before bed. "I'd have to move it before I'd go to sleep. I never put it down without reading the Bible first. If it hadn't been there, I probably wouldn't have messed with it."

On Sunday afternoons, relatives and neighbors often gathered at the Moores' house. His mother and other moms would make ice cream on the porch while the kids played in the fields. Once his dad got sick with the mumps and had to spend two weeks in the hospital. The timing was terrible because the crops had to be harvested. The neighbors, realizing the dire situation, brought in the crops without telling G.A.'s dad. When his father got out of the hospital, he looked across the fields and broke down in tears. "He walked behind the mulberry tree and sat down and cried. It was the only way he could express the love and thankfulness he felt toward his friends. That's the kind of neighbors we had. Boy, I was blessed to grow up with such great, great people."

His father passed away in 1979 at the age of sixty-six. He was breaking a horse for G.A.'s son, who was then only two. The horse threw him off, and he landed hard on the ground, breaking several ribs, a hip, and a leg. He also suffered a head injury, and doctors did surgery to remove pressure on his brain.

Doctors warned the family that G.A.'s dad might not survive. He did – for another month. He was improving, but he got a blood transfusion and immediately worsened. Doctors said he had a form of hepatitis, but G.A. later suspected the blood had been infected with the AIDs virus. "Doctors said there was no cure. His death nearly killed me."

***

The broken wrist at North Texas State ended his pro football aspirations, but he fulfilled his second goal when he was hired in 1963 to be the head football coach at his alma mater. Before taking the job, he talked to the superintendent, Ben Smith, who had been the superintendent when Moore was a student. The two had a close, almost father-son relationship. "He told me one time I was the closest thing to a son he ever had."

Smith had watched Moore's performance at Bryson, taking a winless team and earning five victories his first year. He knew Moore could coach, but he worried about the pressure in taking the job. If he didn't win enough games, people would call for his ouster – even though he had starred as a football player at Pilot Point. "Mr. Smith said, 'Hey, I'd love to have you. But coming back to your hometown – I don't know if that's good for you or not. Talk to the board. See what they think.'"

Because he grew up in Pilot Point, he knew all the school trustees. He was especially close to the board president, Junior Cashion, who was a farmer like Moore's dad. In the summers, Moore plowed the fields at Cashion's place, and he paid him a visit to talk about the coaching vacancy. Cashion asked Moore if he thought he could win. "I sure do!" Moore replied. "That's all I want to know," Cashion said. "I'm for it."

Cashion and the other school board members met and voted unanimously to hire Moore. "It was a dream come true," he says. "I wanted everybody to know about Pilot Point as a football town. People in town got excited with me." The local newspaper, the *Pilot Point Post-Signal*, hailed Moore's return as coach. The paper had chronicled his exploits as an all-state running back just a few years earlier, once calling him the "Pilot Point Powerhouse." Moore's hiring made the headlines: "Hometown Boy Returns to Guide Pilot Point." The accompanying article lauded his return: "G.A. Moore, former Pilot Point football star, has returned home to try his hand at guiding the Bearcats back into championship form."

In the early 1960s, Pilot Point had a population of only 1,250. The northeast Texas town, founded in 1866, began to grow in the 1880s after the Texas and Pacific Railway arrived. The town soon boasted several cotton gins, blacksmiths, a hardware store, meat market, and hotel. Many of the stores were congregated around a town square that remains today.

Once hired, Moore started to work immediately, analyzing his roster for the upcoming season. The newspaper, while welcoming Moore back, cautioned that he faced a tough rebuilding job. Pilot Point had captured a district championship during Moore's career as a player in the mid-1950s but hadn't had a winning season since he left. Moore inherited only four returning starters from a team that finished 4-5-1 in 1962. "The task appears pretty formidable, especially for the 1963 season," the paper said. "Moore figures the lack of size, speed and depth will prevent his first edition of the Bearcats from becoming serious title contenders. He's impressed with his charges' desire, however, and this could offset some of the weaknesses."

In an interview with the paper, Moore sounded cautiously optimistic. "We've got a pretty sound first unit, and if none of the boys get hurt we should do OK."

The starting lineup including three seniors: quarterback Mike Enlow, fullback Alvin Evans, and guard Sonny Gibbs. Moore had coached all three of them several years earlier in Pony League baseball. "I knew them all, and they knew me. I inherited a bunch of kids I loved to death." Evans, who still lives in Pilot Point, remembers the first practices under Moore. They were starkly different from the loosely organized workouts of the previous coach. That coach liked to yell more than instruct. "G.A. wasn't the hollering and screaming type," Evans says. "He was a motivator. He could get more out of athletes than you've ever seen. Kids wanted to win for him. As far as his work habits, everything was on time. I mean, boom, boom, boom. He had a schedule made out, and if he says we were going to work on this for thirty minutes, he followed it to the letter."

Gibbs agrees. "I loved playing for him. He coached at a different level than we'd been used to. He was very organized. He blew that whistle, and you moved. He believed strongly in preparation. He wanted you to get tough physically and mentally."

The year before at Bryson, Moore had trouble getting enough boys to field a team. Not at Pilot Point. His roster totaled forty players – plenty of bodies. "We got after it," Moore recalls. "Man, I thought it was the greatest thing in the world. I worked my tail off, but it wasn't work. That first year, I had so much fun."

In the opening game, Pilot Point faced Muenster, which had clobbered the Bearcats the previous season. This year, Pilot Point dominated, winning 58-28 at home. Players and fans carried Moore off the field to celebrate the win. The Moore Era had begun in high fashion.

"Moore turned loose a bevy of jackrabbit backs and a deadeye passer in getting his first victory before the home folks," the *Post-Signal* wrote. "Each of the starting backs scored twice as the Bearcats rolled up 301 [yards] rushing and 223 by air. The game was never in doubt after the opening period, when Pilot Point scored 22 points."

The players "busted their tails," Moore says. "They played above their heads." In the second game, Pilot Point beat one of its biggest rivals, Celina, 22-12. With a 2-0 start to the 1963 season, Moore and his players had plenty of confidence, but their swagger took a blow with a 15-14 loss to Whitewright in week three. Moore and the players remember the narrow loss painfully. Late in the game, Evans carried the ball three straight times from the one yard line. Each time, he says, the ball crossed the goal line for a touchdown – but each time, the referees ruled he came up just short.

The game was played in Whitewright, and Evans is convinced the hometown referees conspired to deprive Pilot Point of victory. "It was such a heartbreaker, knowing we won that game. I never forgot it." Moore questioned the officiating too but says Pilot Point should have scored several times earlier to seal the deal. "Then we wouldn't have had to worry about that one point."

For the fourth game, Pilot Point returned home and whipped Sanger 12-2. Excitement grew among the players and fans. "With a 3-1 record, the Cats are considered strong contenders for the District 15-1A championship," the *Post-Signal* proclaimed. Then the team faced an opponent it never could have imagined – one that wasn't on the field. An illness, originally thought to be mononucleosis, swept through the school. It caused dozens of kids – including several football starters – to miss classes. Officials cancelled football practice and the next two games. "The doctor came in and quarantined the whole football team," Moore says. "It scared everybody to death."

The newspaper described the situation ominously: "Four boys, all football players, and one girl are reported definitely to have the glandular fever – infectious disease accompanied by high fever and swelling of the lymph glands and typified by an abnormal lack of energy. Seven other members of the football team also showed symptoms of the disease when given tests Wednesday."

Two weeks later, another doctor examined the students and determined that they did not have mono but a less serious virus, and kids were cleared to return to class and practice. "Nine starters had been affected, but Moore said Wednesday that they were ready to get back to work," the *Post-Signal* reported. He feared the two cancelled games would hurt the team's momentum, but in its first game back, Pilot Point defeated Wylie, the preseason district favorite, 27-24. "We played pretty dern good," Moore says. In close games such as the one against Wylie, Moore often delivered rousing halftime speeches that lit a fire under his players. "I'll never forget those speeches," Evans says. "Sometimes, a tear would come to your eye, you were so motivated. You wanted to tear the damn stadium down."

After the Wylie win, Pilot Point's record stood at 4-1. The next game would be at home against Frisco, its biggest rival. Moore wanted to win – no, he *expected* to win. Instead Frisco prevailed, 6-0. "Boy, that just about killed me and our kids too," Moore says. "It broke their heart because they wanted to win so badly. It was really hard to accept. I still think we had a better ball club." After the loss, Moore was approached in the locker room by Smith, the superintendent. He wasn't smiling. "I'd like to see you in my office," Smith told him. Moore feared the worst. "I thought he was going to fire me."

Moore walked across campus, his heart racing, to the superintendent's office. He opened the door – and saw three familiar faces. They were longtime family friends and fierce supporters of Pilot Point football. Instead of criticizing Moore, they wanted to assure him of the town's support. Smith smiled as they talked. Relieved, Moore sat down and regained his composure. "It was such an uplifting thing for me. Those guys were my heroes when I was playing because they were at every game. It didn't make any difference where we were playing. They were going to be right on the sidelines, hollering the whole time. For them to say, 'Hey, we're proud of you' was really special."

Moore then led his squad to a 25-14 victory the next week over Princeton. Enlow and Evans each scored touchdowns. In the final two games, the Bearcats split to finish 6-3. Moore had hoped for a better record, but fans and players were delighted. He had rekindled enthusiasm for football and won the devotion of his players.

"Coach Moore knew how to handle people," says Enlow, the quarterback. "I heard that in his later years, he was pretty strict. But I never thought of him as being real strict. He sort of took me under his wing. He educated me on what I should do, like get rid of the ball when nobody's open. If I did something wrong on the field, when

I came to the sideline, he'd tell me about it – and that was all there was. He never screamed at me at all.

"Something about him made him different from all the other coaches I played for. He just had the quality to get the best out of everybody. I loved playing for G.A. I have all the admiration in the world for him."

***

Moore felt confident heading into his second year as Pilot Point coach in 1964. The local paper noted with excitement that a record sixty-five boys reported for two-a-day workouts in August. "Eleven of those are returning lettermen, and four were all-district last year." The first game, however, was a letdown. St. Mark's, an exclusive Dallas private school, walloped Pilot Point, 36-6. Moore's squad recovered and reeled off four consecutive victories, including a 34-0 shutout of Era. Two losses, however, followed. In the final three games of the season, Pilot Point plowed over opponents to finish 7-3. The record was a slight improvement over Moore's first year at Pilot Point but not enough to win the district.

The 1965 season was memorable for two reasons. First, Pilot Point High School integrated racially. Second, Moore won his first district title, finishing 8-0-2 to advance to the playoffs. Across the country, integration was met with strong resistance and even violence in some places, but in Pilot Point, blacks and whites attended class and played sports together with little tension. Moore thinks he knows the reason. Pilot Point was a poor farming community with little gap between the "haves" and the "have-nots." Black and whites often worked the land side by side. "Integration was no big deal for me. We already had a relationship."

In many parts of Texas, however, blacks were not welcomed onto football teams. They played at segregated schools with inferior equipment and fields. Black schools were overseen by a different state governing body than white schools, and the exploits of black players didn't receive the same attention as those of whites. However, the schools produced extraordinary talent. The players from the segregated schools who later starred in the NFL include Joe Greene, Ken Houston, Harvey Martin, Bubba Smith, Charley Taylor, Otis Taylor, Duane Thomas, and Gene Washington.

"We were in our own world," one player, Johnny Kennard, told the *Dallas Morning News* in 1999. "We would often wonder what it would be like to play an all-white team. In the back of our minds, I think we believed we could beat them."

In Pilot Point, Moore welcomed black players onto the football team and made it clear he wouldn't tolerate any racial problems. A team photo from 1965 shows that six of the twenty-four players were black. One was wide receiver Tommy Johnson, a junior when the high school integrated. Previously he and other black students in Pilot Point endured an hour-long bus ride to an all-black high school in a nearby town. For the first time, Johnson and other blacks could walk to school. He says he liked Moore and never encountered any mistreatment from him or white players.

"If you were good enough to play, you played," Johnson says. "G.A. was a lot of fun to play for. He was a young coach, and he got in there and jumped up and down. He was real excited, and he got the team real excited. Integration wasn't that bad in Pilot Point. There wasn't that much tension. We were all farmers at that time. We were all pretty well equal."

Black players in Pilot Point may not have encountered racism from their teammates, but they did from opposing teams. Johnson remembers a game early in the 1965 season against Whitesboro, a team with no black players. Some Whitesboro fans threw objects at the Pilot Point black players and used the N-word, he says. "It was kind of rough," Johnson recalls. "It shocked us, but we handled it. G.A. talked to us. He said, 'Don't get upset. Don't pay it any attention. We came here to play football, not to cause any trouble.' Before games, he'd sit us down and say, 'We might have some problems out of this town. But don't pay no attention to what they're saying.'"

Andrew Johnson, a cousin of Tommy Johnson, says the black and white players became like a family. "We had hauled hay together and worked in the fields together. We used to play touch football in the field across from my house. The whites would come down and play with us."

Gary Bruce, another black player, says Moore took a personal interest in each player, black or white. "I always wanted to play for him. There was just something about him. We were small and didn't have a lot of talent, but he'd mold us into great teams. I loved his style of football. He'd run quick plays, reverses – things other coaches weren't prepared for. He always caught someone off guard. He checked our grades to make sure we kept them up. He didn't just care about football. He cared about being a good young man and building character. I still call him coach. He'll always be Coach Moore to me, never G.A. That's out of respect."

The black athletes played a critical role in the team's success in 1965. The team had lost seventeen players to graduation the previous year. Six of those were all-district. The *Post-Signal* had picked Pilot Point to finish fifth in a six-team district, but Moore quickly sent a message to naysayers. Pilot Point rolled over Valley View, 44-0, in the opener and won its next two games as well. Two ties followed, but in the final five games, Pilot Point went undefeated and notched two more shutouts, 42-0 over Princeton and 39-0 over Frisco.

The Frisco win was particularly rewarding. Both teams, longtime rivals, came into the game without a loss. Frisco had won twenty straight district games and four consecutive district titles. Pilot Point took a 12-0 lead into halftime and then piled on more points in the second half. Frisco coach Lloyd Nichols came to the Pilot Point locker room afterward to congratulate Moore and the players. "I just wanted to tell you that you gave us a good old country licking," Nichols said. "You did a good job, and we have no excuses at all."

In the final game of the year, Pilot Point thrilled home fans with a 53-12 victory over another longtime rival, Celina. The win sealed the district title. "The Bearcats displayed fantastic prowess in the realm of broken field running and were virtually unstoppable every time they got a little running room," one newspaper article said. Another praised the team: "The coaching, quarterbacking, passing, blocking and rock-'em, sock-'em defensive play that has prevailed during the season has given Pilot Point a team to be proud of." The paper ran a photo of the flat-topped Moore in a white dress shirt, skinny tie, and sport coat in the team's locker room after the win. "All of them gave one hundred percent all of the year," he said. "I don't think we have any particular standouts. We have twenty-five boys on the A-team, and all twenty-five play."

The excitement of winning district, however, didn't last long. In the first playoff game, Pilot Point lost to traditional powerhouse Honey Grove 30-14. The Bearcats scored first on a seventy yard punt return, but Honey Grove dominated the rest of the game to advance. In 1966, Moore hoped to build on the success. Instead the team faltered. Pilot Point lost three of its first five games, rebounded slightly, and then lost the final game to finish a disappointing 5-5. The next year wasn't much better. Pilot Point wound up 5-4-1. Moore felt intense pressure, not from others, but from himself. He thought he wasn't giving the town the winning team it deserved.

In 1968, however, Moore led a resurgent team that finished 10-0 to win the district title. In the opening game, Pilot Point beat Celina 6-0, on a play that infuriated the opposing coach. Moore, always looking for an edge, called a "hideout play" – a ploy that has since been banned. A player lines up on the sideline facing the coach, instead of being with the other players. When the ball is snapped, the sneaky player races down the field and looks for a pass. On the winning play against Celina, the hideout receiver was Butch Ford, a star running back who would later spend twenty-five years as an assistant coach under Moore. Ford scored from sixty-five yards out to supply the margin of victory.

The Celina coach, Virgil Miller, still remembers the play. He and Moore are close friends, but he's adamant that the hideout play shouldn't have counted. It wasn't illegal at the time, but Ford, eager to get a head start, lined up offsides, Miller contends. "We tried to call it to the officials' attention, but I don't think they saw it. It was the first year we had video, and the game film showed it. We had them red-handed, and G.A. knew it." Days after the game, Miller was still hopping mad. He finally persuaded Moore to come tell the Celina players that Ford was, indeed, offsides. Moore did so grudgingly: "'The play was illegal, but what's happened has happened.'" Miller admired the coach's admission: "G.A. is a real gentleman."

Most of Pilot Point's other wins in 1968 were by much larger margins than the 6-0 triumph over Celina. The Bearcats pounded Whitesboro 63-0, Sanger 54-0, and Royse City 40-0. In the final regular season game, the Pilot Point offense exploded, rolling over Farmersville 72-25. "We just got better and better and better," Moore says. "We had a backfield as good as any in the state."

The stage seemed set for a deep run into the playoffs, maybe even a state championship. The Bearcats' first-round opponent was a familiar foe, Honey Grove. In Pilot Point's last trip to the playoffs in 1965, Honey Grove downed the Bearcats 30-14. This time, the two teams seemed more evenly matched. For instance, Pilot Point had scored 426 points in its ten regular season games, compared with 414 for Honey Grove. On defense, Pilot Point had given up only fifty-nine points all season, compared with fifty-four for Honey Grove. "The two teams are just a whole lot alike," Moore said before the game.

Pilot Point, however, suffered another playoff disappointment. This time, Honey Grove won, 13-6. The game was closer than in 1965, but the sting of defeat was just as sharp. Quarterback Steve Coffey threw an interception late in the game when Pilot Point had moved to the Honey Grove twenty yard line. Coffey imagined leading his team to the winning touchdown. Instead Honey Grove picked off his pass near the sideline and returned it eighty-five yards for the clinching touchdown.

"It was in my hands, and I didn't get the job done," says Coffey, who still lives in Pilot Point. "It's that simple. G.A. never blamed me for anything. He never would have done anything like that. He's a real Christian man, and he cared for everybody. I guess that's why everybody played so hard for him. You knew in your heart he loved you."

Four times in the first half, Pilot Point advanced inside the Honey Grove twenty yard line but managed only one score. Junior Worthey, a standout tackle for Pilot Point, remembers Moore's speech after the bitter loss. "He was pretty down," Worthey says. "But he just told us to accept it, that it was part of life, that there was a reason for it. He says he felt sorry for the seniors but that the juniors would just have to regroup and try again next year."

In the next two seasons, however, Pilot Point didn't return to the playoffs. In 1969, the Bearcats had a strong team, finishing 8-2. But narrow losses to Celina in the first game and Farmersville in the last kept Pilot Point from winning the district. In 1970, Pilot Point opened with a 53-0 thumping of Southlake Carroll, but two slim mid-season losses – 14-13 to Frisco and 16-14 to Nocona – hurt its playoff hopes. The Bearcats ended the season with another narrow defeat, 18-15 to Lake Dallas, to miss the post-season.

Today the Texas high school playoff structure allows the top four teams from a district to make the playoffs, but in the 1960s and '70s, when Moore compiled many of his wins, only the district champion advanced. Those razor-thin losses that Moore suffered, haunted him. He wondered how many playoff games, and even state championships, the Bearcats could have won if they had captured more district titles. "If I could have done a little better job of coaching or preparing those kids, we would have won. That still bothers me."

After the 1970 season, Moore left Pilot Point. He wasn't forced out – far from it. He was still viewed as a local hero – a standout player who returned home to build a winning program. Moore didn't leave Pilot Point to take another coaching job. He left, he believed, to follow God's calling into an entirely new direction.

In His Own Words...Character Matters

TD Celebrations

We handed the ball to the official when we scored. You don't have to showboat and throw your hands up and do all the stuff they do in the pros. Everybody knows who scored the touchdown or made the tackle or intercepted the pass. You're just drawing attention to yourself. It takes away from the team. There's a difference in the way you act when you're a winner and you expect to win. It goes back to leadership, and it reflects on the coach when you do that kind of stuff.

I had a boy try that once. He kind of high-stepped the last three or four steps into the end zone. It was probably the first touchdown he ever scored. We took him in a room by himself at halftime and had a little talk with him. We told him, "You won't ever set foot on the field if you do that again." He didn't understand at first, but he wound up understanding. He never did that again. That was his junior year. He wound up being an all-district wide receiver. He's one of my best buddies right now.

Football's Life Lessons

In football, you get knocked down more than in anything else. You have to get back up and keep going. People who are going to come out ahead keep getting up and getting up and getting up. You learn so many things from it. You have to sacrifice and work if you're going to be good. Things are not always going to go right in a football game; they're not always going to go right in your life.

I can still remember high school games when I played – everything about them. I heard one guy say, "I may have trouble remembering my wife's name every day, but I can sure remember my football games when I was in high school." That's the kind of impression it makes on you.

Gentlemen

On the field, we want very aggressive personalities. Outside the white lines, we expect perfect gentlemen. Many times, players get confused. They are aggressive off the field and very meek on the field. The ultimate compliment is for faculty members or people in the community to say, "He is too nice to be that guy I watch on Friday night."

Leadership

When you've got fiery leaders that helps. I remember one time we had a tight end who was great, but we had a big ballgame coming up, and he wasn't working out as hard as he should have been. One of our running backs took him outside the building when we had a water break and hit him in the mouth. I mean, just decked him. He told him, "Get your tail after it! Get to work!" Now, we don't tell them to do that, and I got on them bad for that. There's better ways to settle it. But this kid thought that's what he needed to do. We won state that year.

Cussing

We don't cuss players. I might say crap – that's probably the worst thing I ever said. That's just the way I was raised. I don't think you need to cuss them. My high school coaches didn't cuss. When I got to college, I had one that talked to us pretty straight, but I don't think you have to do that.

Distractions

We asked the players to put football first. Every year, I'd say, "There's nothing wrong with having a girlfriend, but I expect you to be home at night studying about the football game, not talking on the telephone with her." They'd slip around. We're not dummies. We know what they're going to do. This texting about ruined me. When they were juniors, we gave them letter jackets. I told them, "If you give your jacket to a girl, we're going to get it back. When you graduate from high school, you can do whatever you want with that jacket, but as long as you're in school, they won't be wearing them up and down these hallways." Those gals didn't play football. You've got to have pride in them things. You don't give away things you've got pride in.

Selfishness

If there's one word I hate in coaching or life, it's selfishness. Selfish people cause more problems in this world than any other group of people, I think. Selfishness and team cannot exist. We will eliminate a selfish star to keep a team.

Cutting Players

We never cut anybody. I don't think anyone's smart enough to look at a kid when he's a freshman and say, "Hey, you're not going to make a player." You can tell a stud. You don't have to be no Einstein to do that. But I've seen kids that were just ridiculously pitiful that worked their tail off and made themselves into ballplayers. You stay in that weight room and you do your running – you're going to get stronger, and you're going to get faster. We'll find a place for you to play a little bit. I had one kid who I never thought would play a down, and he wound up being an all-district center. He couldn't outrun Lois Ann [my wife]. He could hardly walk. But he could snap the ball and block and grab because he wanted to play so bad. If I was going to cut somebody, I would have cut him. I loved that kid to death.

Loving and Supporting the Kids

I think I've told every kid I've coached that I loved him. That's the way I felt. I really did love them. I loved all these kids whether they were great athletes or not. Now that doesn't mean you aren't going to get on their seat, but it means they know that you really care about them. Hopefully, they'll have some good memories of when they were in high school playing football. I hope I didn't tear too many of them down. I don't think I did. I got on them pretty good if they fumbled or threw an interception or missed a tackle. But at the same time, I think they knew I really cared about them. Kids would even stay at our house a lot. They'd come out and sleep in the loft in the barn. The big thing was, them suckers always knew there was something to eat. In the middle of the night, you'd hear the backdoor open. They'd have a flashlight, and they'd be slipping in there to the icebox, getting them something to eat at midnight or one o'clock in the morning. Lois Ann would just laugh. We knew they were doing that. We had quite a few kids who'd stay with us the night before the game because they were in a pretty bad home situation.

For the last thirty or forty years, we had a swimming pool, and we had kids in the pool all the time – not just football players, but everybody in the whole neighborhood. If you're in the school business, you need to be taking care of kids. Some of the kids I spent the most time with didn't play football. I went to all the girls' activities, the band activities. I was real involved with it. I went to all the stock shows in Celina and Pilot Point. You don't see many coaches do it, but I was raised here. I knew everybody in school and everybody in town.

Start Them Young

We put some of the best coaches to work with the junior high because, to me, that's the most important part. If a program is going to be good at the top, it has to be good at the bottom. At junior high, the players learned all the things at an early age we expected them to do in high school. They ran the same offense and the same defense. They said yes sir and no sir. They wore their hair a certain way. They looked like a team. They *were* a team. When they got to high school, we didn't have to teach them any of those things. They knew them.

Teammates Stick Together

Here's one thing that shows you how close we were: Maurice Irvin, one of our best running backs, died a few summers ago. He was a senior in 1968. He played college ball and was outstanding, then he wound up being a highway patrolman for years. I did the service. At his funeral, the pallbearers were the starting backfield from high school, plus Junior Worthey, a lineman. Every senior player except one was at the visitation on Wednesday or the funeral on Thursday. Folks, that's a long time ago. That shows you, I think, a little about the camaraderie that develops among teams, especially teams that win. Teams that win stick together. Something about winning brings you closer together.

Kids Haven't Changed

To me, kids are about the same. They still want somebody to make them act right, and they want somebody to love them. You know, pat them on the back every once in a while, but at the same time have some high expectations for them.

Chapter 4
<u>A Higher Calling</u>

G.A. Moore loves the Lord.

He has his entire life – ever since he walked the aisle of Mustang Baptist Church as an eight-year-old and accepted Jesus as his savior. Growing up, he read the Bible regularly and never missed church. In college, he served as Sunday school superintendent while managing his course load and playing football.

Before making any major decision, Moore prayed for guidance. He prayed before taking his first coaching job in Bryson. He prayed before taking his next job in Pilot Point. He always tried to follow God's direction for his life, but after eight years in Pilot Point, Moore began to wonder if it was still God's will for him. Sure, he had enjoyed outward success, leading the Bearcats to two district titles and a stellar record of 56-22-3 – while preaching the value of hard work, discipline, and accountability.

Yet he questioned if the Lord have something else in mind for G.A. Moore. He asked himself that question over and over in his final year at Pilot Point in 1970. The questioning intensified the following spring when he suddenly became ill and lost twenty pounds. A doctor diagnosed Moore with mononucleosis and ordered him to stay in bed for two weeks. During this time, he felt God speaking to him as never before.

"Those were two of the toughest, yet most enlightening weeks of my life. God received my undivided attention. I knew God was calling me to do something different. This was a big surprise because I loved coaching football, but the more I lay there, the more I thought and prayed. God convicted me and pointed out that I had put football too high in my pecking order. I asked God to forgive me, and I felt Him calling me into ministry. I'd put football ahead of everything else, and it was time to get my priorities lined up right."

When Moore recovered, he sought out Wilbur Carter, his pastor at Calvary Baptist Church in Pilot Point. The two prayed – not just once, but several times, repeatedly asking for guidance. One day, he and Carter got in Moore's pickup and took a drive in the country. They talked for hours. Moore felt a stronger and stronger pull toward the ministry, but he wanted his pastor to confirm that the stirring was from the Lord.

"From everything I can observe, I think you're right," Carter told him. "I think you're being called into the ministry."

"OK, I'm ready to do it."

Just like that – after a lifetime of pursuing football as a player and a coach – Moore was prepared to walk away from his passion and follow another direction. Now he needed to tell his wife, Lois Ann. They two had few secrets, but Moore hadn't told her about his thoughts of entering the ministry. He wanted to make sure he was hearing the voice of God before he proposed such a dramatic career change. "I had no idea what her reaction would be."

He sat down with her at the kitchen table, a spot where they often had their best talks. He got right to the point. "I feel like we're being called into the ministry." He remained silent, waiting for her reaction.

"If you feel like that's what we need to do," she replied, "let's do it." Moore felt an enormous sense of relief. He needed Lois Ann's affirmation, and he had gotten it. The two prayed together and grew excited about the new path ahead.

First, though, Moore had to tell his boss, Ben Smith, that he planned to resign at the end of the school year. Smith had been Pilot Point superintendent when Moore attended high school in the mid-1950s and was still superintendent when Moore came as coach in 1963. "He was like a dad to me. I went into his office and told him my story. I told him I needed to resign as coach."

Smith replied, "If this is really what you think you need to do, then I'm for it. But let me tell you something: You can touch more lives as a Christian coach than you can as a pastor."

His words penetrated Moore. Was Smith right? Was his calling really on the field, not in the pulpit? Briefly Moore questioned his decision. Anxiety gripped him, but a few minutes into their conversation, his conviction to enter the ministry returned and grew stronger. He turned in his resignation without any doubt.

Moore needed to save money to attend a Baptist seminary in Fort Worth, an hour away. A lifelong cowboy, he entered several rodeos, hoping to earn a windfall in prize money. His best event was calf roping, but for all his love of rodeoing, he didn't have the talent to win big. "I made enough money to pay for the entry fees, but not the gas. The Lord showed me pretty fast I wasn't that good."

So now he needed another way to make money to pursue God's calling. He heard about a junior high principal's job in Celina, another small town only twelve miles east of Pilot Point. Lois Ann was teaching elementary school there. He figured the two could ride to school together in the fall and save money, and by spring he would have enough for seminary. He accepted the job. When school started, Moore went from being "Coach Moore" to "Mr. Moore."

The transition from coach to administrator felt comfortable. "I knew in my heart that finally I was doing what the Lord wanted me to do."

Moore roping a calf on his ranch, 1970

When the football season started, Moore unexpectedly found himself in the press box. The coach, Gerald Browder, knew of his background and asked him to help analyze the opposing teams. Moore liked being back in the frenzied football atmosphere. He missed it more than he realized – more than he wanted to admit. He didn't question his calling into the ministry, but he felt conflicted at times. The football team did well and advanced to the playoffs. When the season ended, Browder resigned – surprising school administrators and supporters. A few days later, the Celina superintendent, Charlie Winfield, approached Moore about the coaching vacancy.

"We need you to help us," he said.

"No, I'm going to seminary," Moore replied. "The decision is already made."

Winfield persisted. "Write down exactly what you would want if you took this job. Then give it to me."

Moore complied, largely out of courtesy. To take the job, he wrote, he'd want the school to hire more assistant coaches, and he'd want to pick them. Plus, he wanted a lighter teaching load so he could concentrate on coaching. The next day, Moore handed the list to Winfield who read it quickly.

"The job is yours," the superintendent said.

"Now wait a minute," Moore said. "I've got to talk to Lois Ann."

How would he explain this turn of events to his wife? He wanted to take the job, but he'd already told Lois Ann – forcefully – that God wanted him to leave coaching and become a preacher. Could he say that God changed his mind? That he was turning his back on God's will? G.A. and Lois Ann rode home from school that day, just as they always did. G.A. worked up his courage to tell her about the coaching job, but she spoke first. She already knew about the offer. The superintendent had told her. Now she wanted to hear from G.A.

"What do you plan to do?"

He gave her the answer he thought she wanted to hear. "I'm still going to seminary."

"I'll tell you what I think," she says. "I think *we* need to be coaches."

Moore was speechless. Then he smiled, grateful and even giddy that Lois Ann hadn't questioned his commitment to God. She hadn't thought he was crazy to return to coaching. She simply confirmed what G.A. already knew: He was a coach, not a preacher. "When she says 'we' need to be coaches, well that settled it. Our marriage took a giant leap upwards."

With his wife's blessing, Moore enthusiastically took the coaching job and went to work. Fortunately he didn't face a rebuilding job as he had in Bryson and Pilot Point. In Celina, the football team had been good for almost a decade. Moore could build on success instead of creating it. He quickly put his own stamp on the team. Just as he had done in Pilot Point, Moore concentrated on teaching and motivating at practice, instead of running the players ragged. He wanted to improve their knowledge, not just their conditioning.

"Coach Moore put a piece of notebook paper on the bulletin board in the locker room," says Keith Scott, who played for Browder and Moore. "It said 3-3:15 calisthenics, 3:15-3:30 special teams, 3:30-4:00 offense, 4:00-4:30 defense, 4:30-5:00 wind sprints. Workouts weren't fun, but we knew there was an end in sight when he mapped them out like that. We knew we were going to be out of there by 5:00 or 5:30 p.m. Coach Moore combined the physical with the emotional and mental aspect."

David Renteria, who also played for both coaches, preferred Moore's softer touch, "He knew how to talk to a kid and inspire a kid. I wanted to do the very best for him." Many players describe how Moore connected with them in a way no coach ever had. He rarely yelled; instead he patiently instructed. He didn't break down players by emphasizing their shortcomings; he built them up by identifying their strengths. Gradually players began to believe in themselves – and they played better than ever.

"He was one of the finest coaches and motivators," says Joey Wester, another player. "He made you want to win. More than anything, he was a great person, a good Christian. If you had any faults, he'd tell you how to correct those faults and make you a better person and a better player. He'd bring out the best in you. He'd say, 'Don't let anybody tell you that you can't do it because you can do anything.'"

Players quickly learned about Moore's faith. He formed a Fellowship of Christian Athletes chapter and encouraged players to participate – although he never demanded it. Moore admired Dallas Cowboys coach Tom Landry, who spoke publicly about his Christianity and was heavily involved in FCA. Like Landry, Moore never proselytized. He had a low-key approach to evangelism, letting his actions speak louder than his words. Wester says he respected Moore's faith and admired the way he taught life lessons to players. He became a father figure. "He made boys into men. I'll never forget him."

Steve Carey, another player, became a leader of FCA. He and others attended FCA meetings at Moore's ranch outside of Celina. Players saw Moore as a man, not just a coach. He created a relaxed, accepting atmosphere that encouraged players to talk about their feelings – perhaps for the first time. "We'd share and sing," Carey says. "Some players who were introverted or had a bad home life said what it meant to be on the team. There was a once-in-a-lifetime spirit there."

***

When the fall season began in 1972, Moore's squad quickly impressed Celina fans. In the first game, the Bobcats shut out rival Pilot Point, 12-0. Moore may have starred as a player at Pilot Point and coached there for eight years, but his allegiance was now with the orange and white of Celina – not the orange and black of Pilot Point. In the second game, Celina was even more impressive, downing Caddo Mills 42-0. The next week brought another shutout: 27-0 over Prosper. After three games, Moore's Bobcats had scored eighty-one points, while allowing zero. He couldn't have asked for a better start, and the football-crazy town buzzed with excitement. In the fourth game, an 8-8 tie to Tom Bean tempered the enthusiasm. The next week, Celina suffered a narrow loss, 14-13 to district rival Anna. In those days, only one team from each district advanced to the playoffs. So a loss to a district foe at the season's midpoint could deal a devastating blow to playoff hopes.

How did Moore's team respond to the setback? By blowing out Blue Ridge 89-0. Fans couldn't remember any Celina team scoring so many points. In the final four games, Celina went undefeated, averaging more than fifty-two points per game. The season had been a tremendous success in many ways, but Moore didn't achieve his goal of making the playoffs. Instead, Anna, which handed Celina its only defeat, took the title.

In 1973, hopes were sky-high for Celina. The local newspaper, the *Celina Record,* said a state championship was a "genuine possibility." The town's support had never been greater. Attendance swelled at the weekly Quarterback Club meetings from a couple of dozen to more than sixty. Members met at 5:30 a.m. each Thursday during football season to eat breakfast and hear Moore talk about the upcoming opponent. The Quarterback Club held work days at the football field, manicuring the grounds, painting the bleachers, and repairing the fences. Members also sponsored fundraisers with the proceeds going towards needed equipment.

As the enthusiasm grew, every home game sold out. Valerie Carey, the wife of former player Steve Carey, was a Celina cheerleader in the mid-1970s. She later returned as cheerleader sponsor. She saw firsthand how Moore influenced the community and built fan support. "G.A. was a master at overseeing the entire program. I think he really understood what a lot of coaches don't – that to win a championship, it takes everybody working together. That means the whole community, the cheerleaders, the mothers, the dads, the Quarterback Club. There was a common goal, a common unity. He made everybody feel that if you didn't do your part, we weren't going to win."

The cheerleaders understood their role: to motivate the players. "There's this thing called Celina Bobcat spirit that descends and makes those boys play better than what they are, and the girls helped create that spirit," Valerie Carey says. "That's what G.A. was a master at – making sure the boys played better than what they were. G.A., probably more so than any other coach, was interested in what the cheerleaders were doing. He could see how to use them to help the team be better. For instance, on Thursday night before a game, he'd have team dinners and invite the cheerleaders – not to serve, but to be special guests, to eat with the team. To be a cheerleader in Celina was an awesome honor."

The players, like the town, backed Moore wholeheartedly. "I would have gone through a brick wall for him," Steve Carey says. "As far as I was concerned, he could do no wrong." Practices, while not overly long, were intense and exacting. Moore would make the offense run plays over and over until all mistakes were eliminated.

"He was a full believer in perfection," says Donny O'Dell, an assistant coach. "We ran the same play until it was just like he wanted it. G.A. was sneaky smart. Especially when he first started coaching, he wouldn't let on that he was very smart. I think he was able to take advantage of some other coaches by doing this." Besides being sneaky smart, Moore could be tough. "He might pull a player off to the side and chew him out up one side and down the other," O'Dell says. "But there wasn't any grabbing the facemask or shaking the helmet. He made you feel like you were worth something."

Moore always made sure his players were prepared for the upcoming opponent. He was ahead of his time when it came to scouting. He had volunteers watch opposing teams to help him develop a game plan that would exploit their weaknesses. "G.A. was a smart man," says Paul Haskell, a former player. "He always put us in a position to win. He could draw up a play and get a score just like that. It didn't take him long to figure out how to beat you. He could see what the defense was doing and make adjustments on the run. At halftime, regardless of the score, we'd make adjustments, and the other team was in trouble. We were a well-oiled machine."

But even after a big win, Celina players never gloated. "G.A. always taught us to be gracious in winning and gracious in losing," Haskell recalls.

Moore started a pregame tradition in Celina that remains today. After the Friday afternoon pep rally, he required the players to stay together until game time. They shared a pregame meal in the lunchroom and then marched to the field house to get taped and have some quiet time for reflection. Moore wanted their minds on football – nothing else. Players didn't talk or cut up. They thought about their assignments and anticipated what the other team would do. As kickoff neared, Moore would address the team. With only a few words, he could whip the team into a frenzy. "Coach Moore was very much into motivation," Scott says.

Even though Moore could be demanding, he had a soft heart. He never cut players who tried out for the team. If they were willing to work hard in practice, they could suit up for games – even if they didn't play a single snap. "He would find a place for everybody," Scott says. "There's one guy in town now who, bless his heart, didn't have the talent to be a football player, but he was on our team. He was a senior, and he traveled with the starters. He didn't contribute anything as far as playing, but Coach Moore included him."

Wester has a similar recollection. "He didn't turn any-body away. We didn't make fun of anybody on our team because he wouldn't let you. He would take the less for-tunate and make better people and players out of them."

In the first game of the '73 season, Celina shut out Pilot Point, 12-0 – the same score as the previous year. "The game was not as close as the score indicates," the news-paper wrote. "Celina piled up twenty-four first downs in the game, compared with only six for Pilot Point, and had 361 yards total offense to seventy-three for Pilot Point. Ce-lina struck early in the game with a pair of first period touchdowns and then made them stand up for the rest of the game with a tenacious defense. Moore was compli-mentary of the entire offensive and defensive units, say-ing to single out any individuals would be taking away from the fine team effort the Bobcats put forth."

Celina followed up in week two with another shutout, 39-0 over Caddo Mills. "The Celina Bobcats unleashed all their awesome power Friday night for a 403 yard of-fensive outburst that buried a good Caddo Mills football team," the *Record* wrote. The next week, Celina faced a pivotal game against undefeated Prosper. Although the season was young, the district title could be at stake. Ce-lina came up short, losing 27-19. Just as in the previous year, the Bobcats' playoff hopes took an early blow. Then Celina rebounded, winning the final seven games – most by wide margins. The victories included routs of 82-0 over Celeste, 58-0 over Blue Ridge, and 56-6 over Little Elm. "There was never any doubt in the game's outcome as the powerful Bobcats scored in every period, putting thirteen points on the board in the first quarter for openers," the *Record* said of the Little Elm game.

Celina finished the season with only one loss – just as in '72. This time, though, the Bobcats wound up in a three-way tie for the district championship. A coin toss would determine the winner. Prosper, the only team to defeat

Celina, won the toss. Although Celina failed to make the playoffs again, the season had been a success in many ways. The Bobcats scored 412 points – more than the previous year. And they found a star quarterback: junior Frank Andrews. In the final game, he threw five touchdown passes, bringing his season total to seventeen. Andrews attracted attention because of his performance – and his race. He was black, at a time when few blacks played quarterback.

Moore, who coached at Pilot Point during integration in 1965, always played the best players at any position, regardless of race. In some towns in the early 1970s, a black quarterback would have caused a fuss, but not in Celina. Moore's influence prevented any racial discord on the field or in the stands. "Coach Moore gave everybody a chance," Andrews says.

Pat Hunn, Andrews' backup, was white. Hunn never doubted that Andrews, a better runner and passer, should be the starter. The two became close friends. "Coach Moore was ahead of his time with black quarterbacks," says Hunn, now the public address announcer for Celina football games. "He was basically about winning ballgames and putting his best athletes at quarterback."

Moore preached toughness to his players – both mentally and physically. To prepare them mentally, he gave them written tests before each game to make sure they knew their assignments. If they didn't score well, they didn't play. "He convinced us every week that, if we didn't have our 'A' game, we were going to get embarrassed," Hunn says. "He was a psychological master. He wanted you to be smart, to know your offense." To develop physical toughness, Moore employed a number of drills, such as "bull in the ring." In the drill, a player stood in the center of a circle, and Moore called on others, one by one, to charge him. The two players squared off, hitting with their shoulder pads, helmets, and forearms to try to drive the other guy to the ground. "If you could knock the crap out of your teammates, you weren't worried about hitting anybody else on Friday night," Haskell says. "We worked out like champions so we eventually became champions."

Perhaps the most famous exercise was called simply the "toughness drill." Moore lined up players four or five across and, on command, ordered them to leap forward at a forty-five degree angle with their arms behind their backs. He wanted them to land on their chest with nothing to break their fall. He watched for players who tried to twist to their left or right to let their shoulder pads absorb some of the blow. "If you're a man, you're supposed to be tough," Moore says. "You're not supposed to be a weenie."

Haskell says the drill worked: "We were boot leather tough."

Several players recall one incident in which a teammate, Steve Harris, did a toughness drill without a facemask. He had a new helmet, and the specially ordered facemask hadn't arrived yet. Moore told Harris he didn't have to do the drill, but he did anyway. No one wanted to disappoint the coach. When Harris launched himself forward, he landed on his nose and chin. He smashed his nose, and his bottom teeth tore through his lip. "Blood was running down his face," Hunn says. But Harris never complained.

Moore had rules for the players on the field and off the field. They included a prohibition on dating during the season. Most coaches wouldn't attempt such an edict, but Celina players largely complied. Or at least they tried to hide their dating from Moore. Sometimes he found out anyway. Several players remember a time when Moore saw them standing with their girlfriends in front of their lockers before school. It was a Friday morning, and a big game was only hours away. "We got caught red-handed," Hunn says. "Boy, he was mad."

Sam Warren, a 225 pound guard, stood next to his petite girlfriend when Moore approached. "He just chewed us out," says Warren. "He said, 'I can't believe you all got girlfriends!'" Moore told the players they weren't focused enough on football and risked losing the upcoming game. The Bobcats took care of business, trouncing the team, but players didn't dare try to make a case for dating. They knew better than to challenge Moore and give the impression they weren't totally committed to Celina football.

Players felt pressure to perform not only from Moore but also from townspeople. The fans, inspired by Moore, also craved football dominance. "If you didn't play well on Friday night, you heard about it at the gas station and the barber shop and the grocery store the next day," Scott says. "People would tell you, 'You need to pick it up. You all didn't look too good last night. You can do better than that.' They weren't being critical – it was just the old school way of motivating you."

Players wanted to please the fans, but they wanted to please the coach even more. "We knew if we didn't win, it would hurt him – maybe more than us," Wester says. "We were just young kids. We didn't realize really what winning was. You really don't at that age. He was a man. He knew what it felt like to win and what it felt like to lose."

Moore loved to win, and when Celina was on a winning streak he became superstitious. For instance, he'd wear the same shirt, pants, and cap as the wins mounted. He also believed in taking a shower just before kickoff.

"I remember one time we were on a Greyhound bus, getting ready to go down to Waco or Waxahachie for a playoff game," says Jerry Moore, a cousin of G.A.'s who was an assistant coach. "The driver says, 'You ready to go?' G.A. says, 'I forgot something. I didn't take my pregame shower.' The boys sat on the bus for about ten or twelve minutes as G.A. went in and took a shower. He got back on the bus and said, 'I'm ready to go.' We went down there and beat them."

***

When the 1974 football season began, Moore was more determined than ever to win a district championship. So were the players. After back-to-back seasons with one loss each, and no district title, Moore and the players aimed to go undefeated. The season, as usual, began by facing Pilot Point. For the third year in a row, Moore beat his former team – this time 28-12.

In week two, however, disaster struck and threatened to derail the season. Celina lost to underdog Allen, 7-6. Allen scored on a long run on the first play and held on to win. Moore was experimenting with a new defensive formation that featured ten of the eleven players positioned on the line of scrimmage. It was a bold, untried strategy. If an opposing runner broke through the Celina line – and got past the only other defender – he could easily score a touchdown. That's what Allen did. Some Celina players questioned Moore's risky defensive formation – privately, of course.

Despite the loss, Moore stuck with the 10-1 defense and tweaked it until it worked consistently. He used variations of the formation throughout his coaching career. Moore liked to put ten men on the line of scrimmage because the offense couldn't block them all. The defenders could swarm runners before they reached the line of scrimmage or tackle the quarterback before he had time to set up to throw. The 10-1 defense was a high-risk, high-reward formation that, when run effectively, allowed Celina to dominate games. Moore loved to dominate.

After the surprising loss to Allen, Moore's players regrouped – as they always did. He taught his teams to be resilient – to learn from a loss but not dwell on it. In the third game, Celina beat Howe 18-0. This time, the 10-1 defense worked magnificently. In week four, Celina downed Princeton 24-13. In the fifth game – the season's midpoint – Celina had its most dominating performance, annihilating Pottsboro 62-0. Moore was never completely happy with his team's play – even when it rolled over an opponent. For example, in week seven, Celina shut out Collinsville 40-0, yet Moore called a meeting of his senior players immediately after the game. Initially they expected to receive praise for a dominating win. Then they noticed Moore wasn't smiling. He was downright surly as he addressed the players. "What's wrong?" they wondered.

They shifted their eyes around the room. Hadn't they just won 40-0? Most coaches would have been elated with the blowout, but not Moore. He saw too many mistakes on the field. He told the seniors that the team had to improve. "We have to play better if we're going to get where we want to get. We're not there yet. We've got to keep getting better!"

"Yes sir!" they replied.

The players later understood Moore's tactic. He didn't want the seniors, the team leaders, to become complacent. He wanted to set expectations higher and higher – to move the bar up, almost out of reach. Moore hungered for a district title, and he wasn't going to let the seniors become content with adequate wins over mediocre opponents. Moore wanted excellence. "It was his way of getting us to think we've got to do better," Carey says.

Players responded to Moore's talk. The next week, Celina ambushed Sadler-Southmayd, 78-0. In the final two games of the season, the Bobcats continued to mow down opponents, beating Little Elm 55-6 and Prosper 66-6. More importantly, Celina won its first district title under Moore, but he didn't let players celebrate for long. The playoffs loomed. In the first game, the Bobcats played like postseason veterans, hammering Lone Oak 54-10. In the second round, Celina kept rolling, beating Paradise 28-7. In the next game, same story: a 49-6 win over Valley Mills. Now Celina had reached the state semifinal game. It was no contest. Celina flattened Lefors 57-6. Next came the championship game. Celina faced Big Sandy, a power-house team from East Texas.

On paper, the two teams looked evenly matched. Each had a powerful offense and stingy defense. Both teams averaged more than forty-three points per game while giving up only about six points. The Big Sandy offense featured all-state tailback David Overstreet, who would later star at the University of Oklahoma and become a first-round NFL draft pick. On defense, Big Sandy had all-state middle linebacker Lovie Smith, who played at the University of Tulsa and later coached in the NFL. "Big Sandy had some studs," Moore says.

Celina, by comparison, had no marquee players. In little Celina, Moore rarely got blue chip athletes who received major college scholarships. Instead Moore developed his winning tradition with undersized players who had oversized hearts. Celina would need all the heart it could muster. The game was played on an unseasonably warm afternoon in December.

Defenses dominated, as the offenses struggled. Big Sandy moved into Celina territory but missed a thirty yard field goal. It then advanced to the Celina one yard line before Bobcat linebacker Scott Tingle intercepted a pass to stall the drive. Celina couldn't move the ball and had to punt. Later Celina tailback Mike Hester broke loose on a twen-ty yard run to the Big Sandy forty-four yard line, but the Bobcats failed to score.

Moore struggled with play calling against the stout Big Sandy defense. Tingle, who also played running back, car-ried in plays to the quarterback, Andrews. Several times,

Tingle remembers, Moore called a play then changed his mind just as he was preparing to run back to the huddle. "In one particular instance, G.A. gave me a play, I turned, and he jerked me back. He gave me another play, and he jerked me back. I was so confused about what play he'd called. When I finally got to Frank, I just called one of our bread-and-butter plays."

Celina got a big break – or so it seemed – in the third quarter. Overstreet was running a sweep to his left, when a defensive end, Steve Harris, hit him and he fumbled. Randy Nelson, an outside linebacker, scooped up the ball on one hop and sprinted seventy yards toward the Big Sandy end zone. "They weren't going to catch me – not that day," Nelson recalls. He got to the end zone, thinking he had scored the go-ahead touchdown. Quickly, however, the referees called back the play. At that time, the rules didn't allow a defensive player to advance a fumble. Instead the team took possession at the spot of the recovery. Apparently other players didn't know the rule either. "One of the guys told me Overstreet got back up and was saying, 'Somebody catch him, catch him,'" Nelson remembers.

Neither team came close to scoring after the fumble, thus the game ended in an unusual 0-0 tie. Before the kickoff, Moore and the Big Sandy coach agreed that if the two teams tied, they would be declared co-champions. Normally the winner would have been determined by which team had the most penetrations into the other team's territory. When the game ended, many Celina players thought they had lost because they knew Big Sandy had more penetrations. They were relieved – but only slightly – by knowing they were co-champs. The Bobcats felt they should have won outright and been the undisputed champions. "We were torn up because we wanted to win," Nelson says. "A 0-0 tie was just no good. The disappointment stayed with us for a while."

Celina High School coaching staff on 1974 state championship team. Left to right: Donnie O'Dell, Jerry Moore, Jerry Jones, G.A. Moore

Moore consoled the players, saying they played hard against a talented foe. Some fans even suggested that Celina should be happy with a tie against mighty Big Sandy. That talk still rankles Nelson. "I knew we could play with them," he says. "I don't think anybody was intimidated by Big Sandy. They probably had more talent and speed than us. We didn't have any superstars – just a group of kids that played well together. That was one of Coach Moore's strengths. He's the best motivator I've ever been around. He could make you believe you could do things way above and beyond your talent."

***

In 1975, the Bobcats aimed to get back to the state championship game – and win it outright. The season got off to a good start with a 33-0 shutout of Pilot Point. Beating Moore's former team had become an annual occurrence by now. In week two, Celina defeated Allen 12-6, avenging its only loss from the year before. The next game, the

Bobcats rolled over Howe 20-0 and they kept on winning the rest of the season, finishing 10-0.

The Bobcats then roared through the playoffs, shutting out their first three opponents. In the fourth game, one step from the state final, they faced Groom. If Celina beat Groom, it could face a possible rematch with Big Sandy for the title. Moore warned his players not to look past Groom. When the game started, the Bobcats were flat. They lost 15-13 on a late field goal.

"As we got into the game, I realized maybe we hadn't prepared as well as we should have," Nelson says. "I don't remember a lot of the game. I tried to put it out of my mind. I do remember Coach Moore calling a timeout late in the game. I was the defensive captain, and I went to the sidelines. I was bawling because I felt like we weren't going to win the game. Coach Moore asked me what was wrong. I couldn't talk. He just patted me on the back and told me to get back in there."

Moore blamed himself for the defeat, as he often did after a loss. "Maybe we got overconfident. That was my fault." Celina had lost many of its best players from the previous season to graduation. It was a credit to Moore's coaching that the team advanced as far as it did in the playoffs. "I think we were playing a lot more on tradition," Nelson says.

The next week, Big Sandy defeated Groom 28-2 to win the outright state title. The much-anticipated rematch between Celina and Big Sandy never occurred. If it had, Celina would have faced a mighty challenge. In 1975, Big Sandy set a national high school record by scoring an astounding 824 points during the regular season and playoffs, while allowing only fifteen points. The most lopsided win: 91-0. Smith and Overstreet returned to highlight the roster filled with stars. Coach Jim Norman says he pulled his studs early in games to keep the scores from getting even wilder.

"If I had left some of those kids in more than a quarter or two, it would have been unreal what they could have done," he told the *Dallas Morning News* in 1999. "They easily could have scored more than one hundred points. That's just the level of talent we had. If anything, I held them back."

In 1976, Moore's fifth season, Celina again had state title aspirations. A district title and a few playoff victories no longer satisfied the team or the town. The new season began in typical fashion   with a lopsided win. Celina shut out Little Elm 42-0. Next Celina beat Frisco, one of its biggest rivals 30-14. Another shutout followed – 21-0 over Anna. The Bobcats ran their record to 9-0. The final game of the season against Pottsboro would decide the district title. Celina's defense played well but not its offense. The Bobcats had a 6-0 lead shortly before halftime and hoped to get another score. With the ball at the fifty yard line, Moore called a sideline pass, but an opposing player intercepted the ball and returned it for a touchdown. "I lost that one for us," Moore says. "It was my fault for calling the play. I remember games like that – ones we lost that we should have won. We won a lot of good ones, and I can remember some of them, but I can remember a whole lot more about ones we lost. If I'd done a little better job of coaching, we'd have won." Pottsboro won 7-6.

Despite the disappointing end to the season, Moore had strong support within Celina and a growing reputation outside of town. Top high school players and their parents began to eye Celina as an attractive place to play. Some parents packed up and moved to Celina so their talented son could be on Moore's team. The numbers were small, but the transfers captured the attention of rival coaches, who accused Moore of illegal recruiting. Some even filed complaints with the University Interscholastic League, the governing body for Texas high school sports. Moore adamantly denied that he encouraged any family to move to Celina, but the rumors grew.

Perry Morris, who was Celina school superintendent at the time and Moore's boss, always defended Moore. "He got accused of all kinds of stuff that wasn't true," Morris says. "All the time I was there, we had families recruit *us*. Some would say, 'I want my kid to play football in Celina.' I'd tell them, 'You can't come here to play football. You can come here to go to school.' Sure, we got reported to the UIL all the time, but we never got in any trouble, so there wasn't anything to it. It was all legal."

Some rival coaches firmly believed Moore was a cheater. "G.A. is well liked here," Morris says. "He's a good Christian man, but he gets a bad rap from outside of Celina. Everybody hates him because they say he cheats. There's no question about it in their minds."

In His Own Words...Understanding Me

Coaching is Fun

I had a lot of fun coaching for a long time. Coaching football, to me, is not working. How lucky can a man be when he gets to do something he loves doing every day and gets to do it for years and years and years. I've been awfully lucky and awfully blessed. I ain't got no business winning eight state championships. *I* didn't win them – I can say that real quick. But I was part of it. I got to be part of all the good things that took place.

Focusing on Work

I never played golf because of Bear Bryant. I listened to him talk one time at some clinic down at the Baker Hotel in Dallas years ago. He said, "All right, we're at coaching school. How many of you suckers brought your golf clubs?" About three-quarters of them raised their hands. He said, "Well, let me tell you something. I don't play golf. If you'll show me a head football coach who shoots par golf, I will show you a football team I want on my schedule – because I'll be working while he's playing golf." So I never played golf.

Expectations on a Coach

Pressure is part of coaching. You expect pressure. You want it. You don't want to coach in a town where they don't expect you to win, where nobody cares.

Regrets

We won some games, and I'm awfully proud of that. But the ones I think that really stick with you are the ones you lose. You go back and think, I should have done something to keep us from losing this ballgame. I used to stay up all night after a loss, figuring out what I could have done differently. I figured it was my fault more than the players. I don't think you go around blaming players. Coaches are the ones supposed to get them ready to play.

The thing that bothers me is looking at how many games we lost by one and two points back in the sixties. A bunch of them were last games. You don't lose them last games. You have to win state not to lose the last game. If I had just been a little better coach, if I had done something a little differently, we might have won those ballgames.

My Mentor

Tom Landry was always my hero. He was a guy who showed me you could do things the right way and still win. I spent a week with him in 1968 in Estes Park, CO, at a Fellowship of Christian Athletes conference. That's where I got to know him. That was the first FCA camp I'd ever gone to. There weren't many FCAs back then. I was up there with my family, and we took five boys. We were just getting FCA going real strong, and they were some of our leaders at school. We had FCA meetings in those days every Thursday morning at my house. We'd watch the *Three Stooges* and eat donuts. We started that about in 1965, but that was the first conference we went to.

Tom Landry spoke up there. I ate with him, and I got up and ran with him. I explained to him what we were trying to do, and he helped me out. When we got back to Texas, he called me up. They had an FCA meeting every two weeks at SMU, and he was the head of it. We'd load all the boys on a school bus in Pilot Point and drive to SMU. They'd always have some SMU players and some of the Cowboys. It really helped me get started in the right direction as far as coaching. I learned you could be a Christian and still win. A lot of people think you have to cheat and cuss and smoke and drink – and he didn't. I was fortunate to be in a position where I got to meet people like that when I was just starting out as a coach.

Recruiting

Anytime someone would move in, I'd get accused of recruiting them. I never recruited anybody. We got turned in every year for I don't know how many years. It never did bother me. I got used to it after a while. People joked about it all the time in Celina.

It was the coaches on the other teams that started it. You'd beat them, and all of a sudden they're saying you recruited those players. That's not right. You need to worry about your own team. A lot of coaches spend more time trying to come up with an excuse for why they can't win rather than being down there working their tail off. I got beat by some good teams, and I never accused them of recruiting.

Growing as a Coach

I'm not near as hard-headed as I used to be when I was young. I don't think I'm any less demanding. I may be a little more understanding because years ago when I first coached, everybody had a home life, a mama and daddy. Now, half your kids you're coaching are from one-parent families. Some are from no-parent families. There just wasn't a whole lot of that back in the seventies and eighties.

Nerves

I think you're always nervous, and you're always uptight. I guess it depends on which game it is. You can be more tight and more nervous. But once the game starts, coaching is kind of like playing. You block everything out and try to just focus on what's going on.

Coaching Again?

I'd love to coach. I'm probably a better coach now than I've ever been. But the only problem is, I always went to school at six o'clock in the morning and came home at six or seven at night. That makes a long day. My legs got tired on the practice field the last few years. I'm not hunting a job. I'm not going to pick up and move. Boy, it'd be fun to coach another twenty years, but I don't guess I will. I'm not even thinking about that, really.

Chapter 5
<u>A Small Town Coach</u>

G.A. Moore could have stayed at Celina as long as he wanted.

In five years as head football coach, he'd built an outstanding program, compiling a 52-5-2 record and winning a state championship in 1974. The 1976 season ended with a disappointing 7-6 loss to rival Pottsboro that kept the Bobcats from the playoffs. But fans and school officials expected Moore to return for a sixth season in 1977 and lead the team back to the playoffs and possibly another state title. Instead the independent-minded Moore accepted a job as head coach at nearby Pilot Point.

Again.

Moore, who starred as a running back at Pilot Point in the mid-1950s, coached there from 1963-1970. He'd taken a miserable football program and forged it into a perennial playoff contender. No one doubted Moore could have success again at Pilot Point, whose fortunes had plummeted since he left, but Moore already had a budding dynasty at Celina with eight playoff wins and a state championship. He had the unwavering support from the small town's residents, who packed the stadium for each home game. Why would Moore leave a great situation in Celina for an uncertain one in Pilot Point?

G.A. Moore could be an enigma. He sometimes would zig when expected to zag. On the field, he might call a risky reverse play when the smart call seemed to be a simple run up the middle. In plotting his career, he'd go against conventional wisdom, listening to an internal voice that others couldn't hear. In 1977, that voice told Moore to return to his roots in Pilot Point. Part of the motivation was to rebuild his hometown team. While Moore was winning almost ninety percent of his games at Celina from 1972 to 1976, Pilot Point won fewer than twenty percent of its games during that same period.

Pilot Point needed some G.A. Moore mojo to revive its program, and its football backers began to court Moore just as a school board controversy erupted in Celina. The board had gone through an upheaval in the mid-1970s over the passage of a $1.4 million bond issue. Detractors mounted a legal challenge to block the building program, which included a new high school, because they considered it extravagant. The court fight lasted until the next school board election, when a slate of bond program opponents won election and scaled back the construction plans.

Moore had always enjoyed the full backing of the board as he built the football program brick by brick into a fortress. Now, for the first time, he wondered if the new, unproven board might question the town's commitment to football. The fighting between the bond supporters and detractors had overshadowed the team – and Moore didn't like that. "Any time you've got controversy, you're not going to do as well," he says. "I always felt we needed to have everybody going in the same direction if we were going to win."

In Pilot Point, football fanatics witnessed the upheaval on the Celina school board – and saw their chance to snag Moore. "Of course, I encouraged him to come back," says L.E. David, who played football with Moore at Pilot Point. "The program was going downhill, and I knew G.A. could bring it back when nobody else could. I liked his discipline, the way he handled kids." David had an extra incentive to get Moore back with the Bearcats. His oldest son, Tommy, would be a freshman in 1977, and his youngest son, Danny Joe, would be in the seventh grade.

The elder David wanted his boys to play for G.A. Moore. No other coach could get as much out of them, he knew.

Morris Morgan felt the same way. His son, Chuck, would be an eighth grader in 1977. He, too, wanted his son to benefit from Coach Moore's football expertise and emphasis on discipline, hard work, and accountability. "A bunch of us talked to G.A. about coming back," the elder Morgan says. "I think they had won only one game the year before." The talking paid off. Moore accepted the Pilot Point school board's offer in early 1977, just in time to begin a rigorous offseason program for the upcoming season. Moore told the local paper he was glad to be back.

"Pilot Point is my home," he said in the *Pilot Point Post-Signal*. "And my ambition when I was in high school was always to coach in Pilot Point. People from around the state used to talk about how good Pilot Point was, and I want it to be that way again. If we get fifteen to twenty [players] who will do everything they can to be the best they can, we'll be winners. It all boils down to the attitude of the players and the town. If the boys have the right attitude, they'll be able to play with anybody in the district. That doesn't mean we'll win every game, but we'll be able to play with anybody."

To the football players, Moore provided needed stability. They had played for one coach who quit after a 1-8-1 record in 1975 and another who was fired after a 1-9 record in 1976. Keith Crutsinger, a quarterback who had endured both miserable seasons, was a junior under Moore in the fall of 1977. "Coach Moore changed the culture and the whole atmosphere in a matter of weeks. It was a remarkable transition. He talked about how important Pilot Point was to him, being a hometown person, and how important it needed to be to us. By the time we got through that spring, we were already doing things we didn't believe we could do. We were a whole different bunch of kids. We felt bigger, stronger, and faster, and we hadn't even put on a football suit yet."

David Carroll, a receiver, also remembers the transformation under Coach Moore. "It didn't take us long to grab the G.A. fever. He's one of those good leaders who make you want to do well. It wasn't long before we saw what he was doing, and we were glad he was there helping us. You wanted to please him. You could tell he cared about individuals. He wasn't self-centered or seeking his own fame. It was all about the team and the town."

Moore crafted intense offseason workouts that included heavy doses of running and weightlifting. He created competition among players to liven up the workouts and test their character. For instance, Moore made "top ten" lists of players in several events, such as the forty yard dash, "400-yard" "gut check," and bench press. Players wanted the praise they received from Moore for making the lists. "We all knew if we didn't work, we weren't going to get on the board," Crutsinger says. "It was a big, big deal. Those lists stayed up in the gym all year long. One of the tributes to Coach Moore is that he already had us competing against each other before we competed against anyone else. He took an average player and made him good; he took a good player and made him great."

Moore says he "worked the players' tails off" in April and May. "That bunch had enough talent to win, but they had never worked out. They did everything we asked them to do." Once players put on pads for two-a-day workouts in August, intense competition began for starting positions. No one was guaranteed playing time, not even returning starters.

"Coach Moore put the best person out there, no matter what," says Danny Scott, a defensive tackle. "It wasn't political. It didn't matter who your daddy was. It only mattered if you could play football. He gave everybody a shot at every position. He wanted the player who would give one hundred percent."

Townspeople were delighted to have Moore back leading the football program, but most didn't expect him to work miracles. After all, the 1976 squad had won only one game and scored a measly 108 points, while allowing 254. Moore had largely the same roster heading into the 1977 opener against Boyd. The outcome shocked people: Pilot Point demolished Boyd 55-6, avenging a defeat from the previous year. Pilot Point raced to a 34-0 halftime lead and amassed almost five hundred yards of offense. "I was tickled with the way we hit," Moore told the local paper after the game. "We're still making mistakes, but we made them going wide open, and that's what counts."

After only one win, the players felt a new sense of pride in being a Bearcat. "When we walked down the hall, our chest stuck out a little further, and our shoulders were a little straighter," Crutsinger says. The players grew together as a unit. "Coach Moore used to always say, 'If you don't care enough about your teammate to jump out in front of a car to knock him out of the way, then you're not the kind of teammate you need to be.' He got us believing that. We were a close bunch of kids – not just at school, but away from school."

Pilot Point followed up the opening win with four consecutive victories, including a 3-0 win over Sanger in the first district game. At the season's midway point, the Bearcats were an unimaginable 5-0. Not only did the players buy into Moore's approach, so did townspeople. Attendance was packed at the weekly booster club meetings and pep rallies. Alois Pelzel, who owned a barber shop on the town square, shut down early on Friday so he could attend the raucous pep rally only hours before kickoff. "I said, 'If you want a haircut, you'd better get here before 3:00.' We closed the town down. We gave them some spirit."

Pelzel, who had a football-playing son in junior high, even volunteered to take part in skits at the pep rallies. He'd dress up like the mascot of the opposing team and then run around the gym as Pilot Point fans tried to catch him. "It was fun," says Pelzel. "I wouldn't take nothing for those days."

Another parent, Joella David, remembers walking through the school hallways on game days with a spirit bell. She and other moms would ring it and do cheers to pep up the boys. Jean Howard, whose son became an all-state center, fostered school spirit in another way. On Wednesdays, she led a group of Bearcat Moms who cleaned the locker room and brought homemade cookies and cakes for players and coaches. On Thursdays, the moms decorated the square with streamers and painted shop windows with encouraging messages for the boys. She even rounded up moms and drove to players' homes to do cheers and sing school songs. "We were just so wrapped up in our kids," Howard says. "G.A. was wonderful. We couldn't have asked for a better role model for the kids. His rules were absolutely fantastic for us because we didn't have to worry about our kids. I guarantee you that the kids who played for him were in church every Sunday. If they weren't, he found out why."

Moore says the enthusiasm among residents helped him build a winning team. "Oh, gosh, I had so much help from all the people in town. That's the only way you can really go in and turn a program around. When you get kids excited and their parents excited and the folks in town excited, then there's an atmosphere they want to be a part of. Coaches don't get it. They think you can sit in the field house and draw Xs and Os and win. But you don't do it that way."

Moore developed a rare bond with his players. He frequently invited them to his house to swim or haul hay. He held Fellowship of Christian Athletes meetings at his house and talked openly about his faith. "He was almost more like a youth minister than a coach," says Chuck Morgan, who played linebacker. "I respected him for his Christian faith more than anything. Even to this day, when there's a funeral in town, you know he's going to be there."

Jerry Price, a defensive end, remembers attending an out-of-town track meet with Moore after the football season was over. Moore, who also coached track, had tried to book enough rooms for all the runners and those who came to watch, but he came up short. Price and two other football players who weren't competing didn't have a room. So Moore invited them to stay in the room he shared with his wife. "One of us had to sleep on the floor, and the other two got the extra bed," Price recalls. "We had a blast that night, just laughing and cutting up with Lois Ann and Coach Moore."

***

In the second half of the 1977 season, the Bearcats struggled. They won two games, while losing three to finish 7-3 and miss the playoffs. All the losses were close, however. Pilot Point fell to Pottsboro 20-7, Celina 21-17, and Aubrey 20-15. Contrast those losses to the 55-11 and 27-0 routs that Pilot Point suffered the year before Moore returned. "We went from Loserville to winning seven games his first year back," says Scott. "Coach Moore brings a community together like nobody I've ever seen. He put one hundred percent of himself into his job. I've heard him say so many times that winning is contagious. Once you get that winning attitude, you learn the things you've got to do. You get your hair cut. You're respectful to teachers. You say yes ma'am and no ma'am. You live by a curfew."

At the beginning of the 1978 season, expectations were high. Eighteen of twenty-two starters were returning, and the Associated Press ranked Pilot Point the state's fifth best 2A team. Moore welcomed the praise but made sure it didn't puff up the players. "You can't pay attention to the ratings until it's all over," he told the *Pilot Point Post-Signal*. "They're just educated guesses by people who feel they know, but there are so many things they can't take into consideration. We can have a good year. We have the talent if everything goes right."

The Bearcats began with a 62-0 thrashing of Van Alstyne, compiling 603 yards of offense and twenty-two first downs. Sophomore Jerome Johnson, who would later earn a football scholarship to the University of Texas, rushed for 144 yards. Pilot Point followed with two more shutouts – 33-0 over Little Elm and 61-0 over Coppell. After a narrow 7-6 win over Muenster in the fourth game, Pilot Point notched two more decisive shutouts, including a 64-0 rout of previously unbeaten Lindsay. Moore always emphasized defense first in coaching.

"I thought if we could keep the other team out of the end zone, we could figure out a way to score," Moore says. "Everyone wants to play offense, but you've got to sell them on defense first. I always told the kids I want a 'hoss' at middle linebacker and a 'hoss' at free safety. And I've got to have two defensive ends who will do what I tell them to do. The rest of the people we can fill in and rotate around."

After winning the first six games of the 1978 season, Pilot Point suffered a painful defeat. Celina, where Moore had coached only two seasons before, shut out Pilot Point 21-0. "I don't like talking about it – even after almost forty years," Carroll says. "Nothing went right that night for us. I can't explain it. We just couldn't move the ball. The guys on the other team were quicker. For me personally, it was like I had lead in my boots."

The Bearcat players paid dearly for the loss. Moore, unhappy with their effort, made them do "toughness drills," or "fronts," at the Monday workout. He had started these punishments back at Celina. He had players line up side by side and leap forward at a forty-five degree angle, with their arms behind their back, so they hit the ground on their chest – with a painful thud. "Oh, gosh, that's one of the hardest things I've ever done in my life," Crutsinger says. "Coach Moore would be in front of us. He'd start tapping people on the helmet and say, 'How tough are you? How mean are you? Can you deal with this?' He'd blow his whistle, and you'd jump as high as you could and land on your belly. You knew exactly how you were going to feel when you touched the ground. And you better not touch your knees. Now people would probably call it cruel and unusual punishment."

Before having the varsity players do the belly-busting drill, Moore called for the junior varsity players to come watch. He wanted to show them the consequence of losing. Greg Pelzel, who was a freshman quarterback, remembers watching the spectacle. "Coach Moore looked over at the freshmen and said, 'If you ever lose a ballgame, you'll be doing fronts.' We made up our mind as freshmen we weren't going to lose any ballgames."

After the character-building loss to Celina, the Pilot Point varsity reeled off three straight lopsided wins to end the season: 42-7 over Callisburg, 49-0 over Pottsboro, and 42-6 over Sanger. The Bearcats finished a strong 9-1 but failed to make the playoffs for the second straight year. Moore had rebuilt the Pilot Point program quickly, compiling a 16-4 record in his first two seasons and flattening most opponents, but he had failed in his goal of making the playoffs. For the next seven years, however, he would achieve that goal and elevate Pilot Point football to new heights.

***

Pelzel never looked like a star quarterback. He stood barely five feet, ten inches and weighed just 165 pounds, with thick horned-rim glasses. He looked more at home in the library than on the football field. In Coach Moore's system, however, Pelzel turned out to be the perfect quarterback. He was smart and could execute plays flawlessly. He didn't have a cannon for an arm, and he couldn't outrun many defenders, but he could read defenses and avoid mistakes. "I understood the game," Pelzel says. Moore hated mistakes. If a quarterback threw an interception or fumbled the ball, the coach never rushed up to reassure him.

"I could never pat them on the back and say, 'That's OK.' It's not OK to make mistakes. You don't fumble. You don't throw interceptions. If you do, you're not going to play. That's just a simple rule. We expect them to be perfect. I'm not ignorant enough to think everybody is going to be perfect, but I'll tell you what – you can play games almost to perfection if you lock in and do what you're supposed to do and practice that way."

Pelzel was only a sophomore when the 1979 season opened, and he didn't start at first. He was a trusty backup who logged considerable playing time when Pilot Point built a big lead, which was often. The Bearcats opened with three straight blowouts – 41-0 over Van Alstyne, 35-0 over Little Elm, and 31-0 over Coppell. When Pelzel became a fulltime starter the next two seasons, he compiled the best winning percentage ever for a Pilot Point quarterback – a record that still stands. He was the type player Moore loved throughout his career: a driven overachiever who made the most of his modest talents. Pelzel attributes his success to Moore's preparation and concern for players.

"He's an incredible individual. He's father-like. He cared about his players and everything that went on in our lives. It wasn't just about football. It was about teaching us life lessons. I know in my household, my parents never set rules for me because Coach Moore set them all. He had a curfew. He didn't want you drinking or getting in trouble. You were supposed to be an upstanding member of the community. Every team has kids who struggle, who don't have good family lives. G.A. was real good about pulling kids into his office and visiting with them. He did a lot of teaching on the field but also in the halls and his office."

Moore could be a kind mentor, but he also could be a demanding taskmaster. Morgan remembers being yanked out of games for missing a tackle or blowing an assignment. "You knew when you messed up because you saw your sub coming in. I always went to the far end of the sideline to try to get away from Coach Moore, but he'd always find you. Most of the time, he'd say, 'You're going to let that boy whup you? He weighs half your weight, and you're letting him whup you!' He expected quite a bit. He knew what every individual was capable of doing."

Individual players may have been whupped occasionally, but the team rolled through the 1979 season with ease. In the eighth game, Pilot Point beat its cross-town nemesis, Celina, for the first time since Moore returned to his alma mater. The next week, Pilot Point stumbled and tied Callisburg 6-6. The Bearcats had five turnovers – uncharacteristic for a Moore team built on avoiding mistakes. "There's not a whole lot we can say about the Callisburg game," Moore told the local paper afterward. "Sometimes it takes something like that to wake you up."

The game did serve as a wake-up call. The next week, in the final game of the regular season, Pilot Point whipped Pottsboro 40-14. The victory gave Moore his first district title in his second stint with the Bearcats. The accomplishment was especially impressive considering that the squad had only six seniors. When the season began, some sportswriters had picked Pilot Point to finish third or worse in the district. "It was other people who were surprised," Moore told the *Post-Signal* after the district championship. "I thought we had a good chance because we probably had the best offseason I've ever been associated with. That is the best indicator you can go by. That's when you win and lose the season."

In the first playoff game, Pilot Point beat Holliday, 14-6 after falling behind 6-0. "The boys never did panic," Moore said afterward. "We were a little tight early in the game. We just seemed to relax and play a little better later on." In the second postseason game, Pilot Point won 20-14 over Wolfe City. With only twenty-six seconds left, Wolfe City had the ball on Pilot Point's one yard line and seemed on the verge of winning the game, but the Bearcats recovered a fumble to secure the victory.

The win set up a hotly anticipated game against China Spring, the defending class A state champion. Moore expressed confidence beforehand. "Everything they do is quick. If we can be as quick as they are and get after it, it will be a heck of a football game. They have a good team, but they're not unbeatable." China Spring's quickness turned out to be too much for Pilot Point in a 20-6 win. The Bearcats gave up touchdown runs of sixty-eight and twenty-nine yards and a scoring pass of twenty-one yards. "We let them make the big plays, and that was it," Moore says. He hated to lose, but he never ripped into the players after a defeat. Moore examined his own shortcomings, rather than blaming players. "I figured it was my fault more than theirs. I don't think you go around blaming players. Coaches are the ones who are supposed to get them ready to play."

When the 1980 season began, the Pilot Point players were prepared. Pelzel, now the fulltime starter, set a clear goal for the team: win the state championship. With eighteen of twenty-two starters returning and confidence from a deep playoff run the previous year, a state title seemed attainable. The Associated Press agreed, picking Pilot Point to take the 2A championship. Moore, as usual, downplayed the preseason praise. "We're not concerned with ratings," he told the *Denton Record-Chronicle*. "They're not going to help us win any games."

Pilot Point, as expected, rolled through the early part of the season, compiling a 5-0 record, including a 30-6 thumping of Celina. He had his team playing "wide open" – one of his trademark phrases. "The average play only takes seven seconds. You've got to sell them on the idea that they can go wide open for seven seconds, time after time after time. If you make a mistake, you want to make it going wide open. We can overcome those kinds of errors, but people who hesitate get beat."

Moore routinely filmed workouts – an unusual practice for coaches at the time. He wanted to point out and correct flaws before they occurred in a game. To prepare his players further, Moore and his coaching staff prepared detailed scouting reports each week on the opposing team. He gave players tests on the reports before kickoff. His message: preparation, preparation, preparation.

"We approached every week the same," Price says. "Even if the other team was 0-6, Coach Moore would say, 'This team can beat you, guys. I promise.' With the scouting report, we knew what our opponents were going to do. We knew the name, number, and tendencies of the guy playing across from us. People don't believe how equipped we were."

During the season, Moore didn't let a rainy day disrupt preparation. He'd take the players inside the gym and let them box against each other. To prevent injury, he had the players kneel and wear oversized gloves. The boxing helped with conditioning and kept the players accustomed to contact. Moore also liked his players to tumble. He put down mats in the gym and had players dive over objects, hit the mat, and quickly get back on their feet.

The tumbling built quickness, agility, and an awareness of their surroundings. "We did tumbling everywhere I've been," Moore says. "We don't want them ever to be on the ground and just lie there."

When the team practiced outdoors, Moore never ended the workouts with wind sprints – a staple of many coaches. Forty yard sprints may build endurance, but they're repetitive and players hate them. Moore achieved the same conditioning results by running plays at a brisk pace or doing drills that replicated game situations. "We tried to make it fun. I didn't think wind sprints were very fun."

When Moore got mad at players – and he did have a temper – he never cussed. His Christian faith kept him from spewing four-letter words, but players distinctly remember him throwing his cap on the ground or popping a player with a towel – just hard enough to convey his disapproval. Most often, however, Moore showed his displeasure with "the look," as players called it. "If you did something wrong in a practice or game, you didn't have to ask if he was upset," Crutsinger says. "His jaw would fix like he was grinding his teeth, and he'd just stand in front of you. He didn't have to say a whole lot because he could get you just by looking at you. I think the kids understood how much it meant to him. When he gave you that look, you weren't just disappointing him. You were disappointing the school, the community, your parents, and everybody else's parents."

His motivational methods worked well throughout the 1980 season. Pilot Point won its final five games to finish 10-0 – Moore's first undefeated season with the Bearcats. The perfect record gave the team confidence heading into the playoffs for the second straight year. The lure of a state title was stronger than ever. In the first playoff game, Pilot Point fell behind to Cooper, 3-0, before rallying for a 14-3 win. The next two weeks, the Bearcats had little trouble – blasting Boyd 51-7 and Moody 40-19. In the semifinal game, Moore's stingy defense rose to the occasion, shutting out Rotan 14-0. "We made a lot of mistakes, and I hope we got them out of our system," Moore told the local paper after the game. "We moved the ball well on them all night; we just made the mistakes at crucial times, and that hurt."

In the state championship game, Pilot Point faced another undefeated team, Tidehaven. The squads seemed evenly matched. Pilot Point had scored more points during the regular season, while Tidehaven had given up fewer points. "Tidehaven is the best defensive team we've played all year," Moore said before the game. "They are bigger than we are and very physical. They are going to give us some problems."

From the start, the game was a defensive struggle. Pilot Point had the deepest penetration of the first half, advancing to the Tidehaven two yard line. On third down, the drive stalled, and Moore opted to try a field goal. A delay of game penalty moved the ball back to the seven yard line. The field goal would still be only twenty-five yards – an easy kick for senior Stanley Hamilton, who had been reliable all year. But he missed to the right.

For the remainder of the game, both teams struggled to move the ball consistently. When the final whistle blew, the game ended in an unusual 0-0 tie. Ironically this was Moore's second scoreless tie in a state championship game. The same outcome happened in 1974 when he coached at Celina. Under current rules, Pilot Point and Tidehaven would have played an overtime period to determine a winner. At the time, however, Moore and the other coach agreed to be co-champions if they played to a tie. The tie didn't sit well with Pilot Point players. "I think we should have won it," Pelzel said after the game. "I don't think anybody in here is pleased. Tidehaven may be, but we're not."

In the decades since the disappointing tie, most players have learned to appreciate the undefeated season and the co-championship. One player, however, still can't stomach the tie. That would be Hamilton, who missed the easy field goal that would have given Pilot Point the outright title. "A lot of people called me 'Wide Right,'" Hamilton says with a half-smile. "I felt terrible. I should have lined up left, and the wind would have hooked it in. There was a terrible crosswind, and in the pregame I was making them."

Hamilton discussed the game during a break from his job at a Peterbilt truck assembly plant near Pilot Point. He's worked there for more than thirty years, along with several teammates. They gathered in the break room to share their memories of the 1980 season and title game. A few minutes into the reunion, Johnny Schindler, a star running back, blurted out, "We got to get to Stan for missing that field goal."

Hamilton groaned. "It'll never die."

The next season, the Pilot Point players vowed to return to the state title game – and win it convincingly. With Pelzel back at quarterback, the offense started the 1981 season in high gear. Through the first half of the season, Pilot Point averaged more than forty-one points per game. In the last five games, the offense proved even stronger, averaging more than forty-five points per outing.

The Bearcats were on a mission. The first playoff game, however, proved the biggest test of the year. At halftime, they led Cooper only 7-6. Moore was steamed with the team's performance. He ordered three leaders – Pelzel, Schindler, and linebacker Danny David – into a bathroom off the locker room for a private meeting. "He lit us up," Pelzel says. "He let us have it with everything he had." The butt-kicking worked. In the second half, Pilot Point pounded Cooper to win, 42-12. "Well, I guess you might say they whipped us pretty good in the first half," Moore told the *Post-Signal*. "We just got together at half and decided we'd go back and do what we were supposed to do. The kids made up their minds to play, and that was all it was."

Pilot Point won the next three playoff games handily to reach the state final for the second straight year. They faced a formidable opponent – undefeated Garrison, whose roster was filled with bigger, faster athletes than Pilot Point. "We had no business being on the field with them," says Mike Russell, an assistant coach under Moore.

To the surprise of most, Pilot Point manhandled Garrison, building an 18-0 halftime lead. Pelzel scored two rushing touchdowns and Schindler one. Early in the second half, Pilot Point stopped Garrison on a 4th-and-1 play on the Bearcats' goal line to keep the momentum. Pilot Point linebacker Rusty Heitzman, who weighed only 147 pounds, managed to make an unassisted tackle on a bruising two hundred pound Garrison fullback. The stop rang Heitzman's bell and left blood streaming down his face. Moore beamed with pride as Heitzman staggered off the field. "I tell you what, I almost cried," Moore recalls. "That was an emotional thing for me, when you see a kid make a lick like that. He knocked the fire out of that guy."

Pilot Point took the ball and drove ninety-nine yards for a touchdown to put the game out of reach. The Bearcats added another touchdown to complete a 32-0 massacre for the undisputed state title. "They had more talent, but we had the better team," Heitzman says. "That's the way it was a lot of times. G.A. was a great motivator in words and actions. He made you play like you were 250 pounds."

Moore remains proud of that championship squad. "They were a team of overachievers. They didn't have any business being as good as they were."

Pilot Point may have had a dominant team, but the individual players didn't attract the attention of college scouts. Only one player from the 1981 team received a college scholarship: Schindler. He played at nearby North Texas State University, now the University of North Texas. He says the college experience paled in comparison to playing for Moore at Pilot Point. "It wasn't even close to being the same. I can remember more games from high school than college. At North Texas, we weren't very good. We were like 2-9 my first year. The crowds were small back then. We probably had more at the state game than at some North Texas games. There was no excitement on campus."

In 1982, the Bearcats hoped for a second straight outright title. It certainly seemed possible. Pilot Point blew through the regular season undefeated, with the closest game being a three-touchdown victory. In the first two playoff games, Pilot Point trounced its opponents. In the quarter finals, the Bearcats fell to Eastland in a cliffhanger 21-20. Not only did the game end Pilot Point's championship quest, it snapped a forty-two game winning streak that stretched over three seasons. "I cried on the field like crazy," says Bill Elliott, who is now head football coach at Celina. "We knew how much it meant to our community. We had worked so hard. Even though I was a freshman and didn't touch the field that night as a player, it devastated me. I couldn't believe we got beat. I remember kind of being in a fog on the field."

In his final three years in high school, Elliott didn't get to experience a state championship. Pilot Point lost in the third round of the playoffs when he was a sophomore, the first round when he was as junior, and the fourth round when he was a senior. That year, 1985, proved to be Moore's last year in Pilot Point. After nine years in his second stint at his alma mater, Moore opted for an entirely new challenge – his biggest yet. He took the head coaching job in Sherman, a much larger school, thirty-five miles northeast of Pilot Point. Sherman played in the 5A classification, the state's largest at the time. Pilot Point, by comparison, played in 2A. Not only was Moore jumping to the big leagues of Texas high school football, he was inheriting a lousy team. Sherman had finished a miserable 0-10 the previous season.

Could G.A. Moore, who had spent his entire life coaching small-town football, make it in the big time? Why would he leave the security of Pilot Point? Part of the reason, he says, is that he had ambitions to coach in college. Shortly before taking the Sherman job, he had applied for the head coaching job at his alma mater, North Texas State University, but was told he needed experience at a larger high school. The Sherman job would let him stretch as a high school coach and possibly open doors to the next level. His college coaching aspirations, however, quickly faded. Once Moore got to Sherman, he says, he realized he was a high school coach through and through. He loved the Friday night atmosphere. He loved the opportunity he had to shape impressionable young men. College could never offer the appeal that he found at the high school level.

***

Moore became aware of the Sherman job because of David Brown, a retired state district judge who was president of the school board and a big wheel in town. It grieved Brown that Sherman football had fallen on such hard times. The 0-10 record in the 1985 season was the worst in school history.

Brown had watched Moore's success in Pilot Point, leading the team to more than one hundred wins and two state championships from 1977 to 1985. Brown thought Moore was the perfect candidate to restore Sherman to the football glory it had enjoyed in the 1970s. All Brown had to do was persuade Moore to leave his beloved Pilot Point High School, where he'd starred as an athlete and achieved icon status as coach. Brown wasn't deterred. "If he wanted something to happen, he was not going to back off until it happened," says his son, Joe Brown, now the district attorney in Sherman. "He was a mover and a shaker. I remember him telling me about Coach Moore's winning record and his reputation."

Judge Brown arrived unannounced at Moore's office one afternoon in spring 1986. Moore didn't recognize the stranger. Brown praised the coach on the jobs he'd done in Pilot Point and Celina and tried to sell him on the opportunity to rebuild a once-proud program at a much larger school. He flat-out offered him the job. Moore, stunned, asked for more time to consider it.

"I'll be back," Brown said.

After he left, Moore mentioned the job offer to his two top assistants, Butch Ford and Mike Russell. Both were intrigued, as was Moore. All three drove to Sherman and scouted the athletic facilities and town. Brown ramped up the pressure by offering Moore a salary of $52,000 – a big jump from the $40,000 he made in Pilot Point. Moore, eager for the challenge and anxious to make more money, took the job. He tried to downplay concerns that he was a small-town coach who might be out of his league. "Coaching football is coaching football," Moore told the *Sherman Democrat*. "There's not much difference coaching 2A than 5A."

Moore took over at the end of the school year. Under Texas high school rules at the time, football coaches couldn't have contact with players in June and July. Moore's first work with his new players didn't come until early August when two-a-day practices began. To make up for lost time, he simplified the playbook and quickly evaluated the talent. On defense, Moore's main message was aggressiveness. Jason Butscher, a linebacker, says Moore once told him to hit opposing players so hard that "snot bubbles come out of their nose." On offense, Moore preached precision. "If anybody missed a snap count, that's one thing that would really tick him off," Butscher says. "He didn't want stupid mistakes. He wanted you to execute. If you missed a snap count, he'd make you run it over and over. If a guy beats you and you're giving one hundred percent, that's one thing. But if you're beating yourself, that used to frustrate him."

Halfway through two-a-days, Moore halted practice and took the boys swimming. He divided the squad into teams and had them compete in relays. Not only did the swimming help soothe their bodies after a week of hitting, it built camaraderie. "Coach Moore was always big about having fun while you were playing," says Troy Davis, an assistant coach. "If you're having fun, you can do amazing things. We sold them on that."

After a second week of two-a-days, the players had bought into Moore's approach. He was no longer viewed as a country coach who wouldn't have a clue at big Sherman. The real question was how the team would perform in its opener against mighty Gainesville, which had pummeled Sherman the previous year. Sherman stunned Gainesville, 10-0. Its swarming defense shut down the explosive opponent. "It was pretty emotional," Moore told the newspaper afterward. "I think these kids realize they can play with people."

The next game, however, proved to be a setback. Denison, the team's biggest rival, steamrolled Sherman, 31-0. The Bearcats managed only sixty-eight yards of total offense and four first downs. The next week, Sherman got back on track with a 37-20 victory over Greenville. A 17-13 win over Weatherford followed. After four weeks, Sherman had an improbable 3-1 record. It was the team's best start in almost a decade. The "crowds and enthusiasm have returned to Bearcat Stadium," the *Sherman Democrat* wrote.

In the fifth game, Sherman suffered a 56-6 blowout loss to Lewisville. Wherever he coached, Moore taught his teams to be resilient – they rarely lost two games in a row. That pattern continued in Sherman. After the disheartening defeat to Lewisville, Sherman reeled off three narrow victories – 15-6 over Wichita Falls Rider, 14-7 over Keller, and 14-0 over Marcus. With two games remaining in the season, Sherman remained in the playoff hunt. The local paper called Moore a "bona fide miracle worker."

Needing two wins to make the playoffs, Sherman got none. The Bearcats fell to Wichita Falls 42-10 and Denton 31-7, but the 6-4 record had been an enormous improvement for Sherman and validation that Moore could coach at the state's highest level. Entering the 1987 season, Moore and the players had lofty expectations. Sherman had some impressive victories and deflating defeats, again finishing 6-4. Players from those teams still marvel at Moore's quick turnaround of the program. "He was a master motivator," says Welby Pleasant Jr., a tackle. "He had a way of communicating to you and getting you to focus in on the task at hand. He could push your buttons to accomplish what needed to be accomplished."

Another player, Lane Aleman, says Moore taught players never to quit. "If you quit on a play, maybe you'll quit on a game. He pushed you. He inspired you to keep working harder. If you work hard, you're going to get rewarded. People talk about luck. The harder you work, the luckier you get."

Chad Points credits Moore with teaching him a valuable lifelong lesson. Before the start of Moore's second season at Sherman, Points decided to quit the team. He was a so-so guard who would rather hang out with his girlfriend than endure a grueling practice. He'd already gotten in trouble with Moore the previous year for wearing an earring to school. Points finally decided he'd had enough of this hard-line coach and his rigid rules. He walked into

Moore's office intent on quitting. To his surprise, Moore wouldn't let him. Most coaches would have gladly gotten rid of a mediocre kid who didn't want to play, but not Moore. He told Points that he'd made a commitment to the team that the other players needed him, and that football should be his top priority. "He told me to get out of his office and meet him on the football field. I was mad at him, real mad."

There Moore ordered Points to do some extra running for having the nerve to try to quit the team. Points took the punishment. He never developed into a star player, but the lesson in commitment and perseverance stuck with him. "If I'd quit, I would have run off with a different group of guys, and who knows what kind of stuff I would have done?"

After high school, Points worked his way through college and law school, never quitting. Today he's a prominent trial attorney in Houston. He credits Moore with giving him the drive to succeed. "As I've grown older, I've realized it was very important that Coach Moore did not let me be a quitter. He didn't give up on me."

***

Moore coached only two seasons at Sherman. He might have stayed longer, but his personal life began to clash with his professional life. Sherman was a long drive from Moore's home outside of Pilot Point – about forty-five minutes. His first season in Sherman, he made the trip every day, leaving about 6:00 a.m. during football season and not returning until about 9:00 p.m. He rarely got to ride his horses and tend to his cattle. The second year, Moore and his wife, Lois Ann, moved to an apartment in Sherman to avoid the long commute. Moore was accustomed to open spaces, and he hated the congested apartment complex. Adding to his worries, his mother, Nell, was growing frail. She had lived alone on a farm near

Pilot Point since G.A.'s dad died almost a decade earlier. With her declining health, Moore was driving back from Sherman often to check on her.

He suddenly had a big decision to make: move his mother to Sherman or move back to his ranch so he could see her every day. As the pressure mounted, another coaching opportunity arose. Celina came calling again. The school board had fired two coaches in two years, and the program was in shambles. Under Moore, Celina won a state championship in 1974 and regularly advanced to the play-offs before he left for Pilot Point in 1977. In the following decade, Celina football had taken a nosedive.

Football diehards reached out to Moore at the same time he needed to make a move. He accepted the job the day it was offered. He welcomed the chance to return to his two hundred acre spread and be close to his mom. "I wanted to get back on the ranch and play with my cows – and still coach football."

In His Own Words...
Dealing with Parents and Fans

Fan Support

Wherever I coached, I had so much help from all the people in town. That's the only way you can go in and turn a program around. When you get the kids excited and their parents excited and the folks in town excited, that's the atmosphere you want. Coaches don't get it. They think they can sit in the field house and draw Xs and Os and win. You can't. No one person can do it. You have to have everybody headed in the right direction.

We started an adopt-a-player program in 1988. That's the best thing we ever did. It's not the mamas and daddies that you need in the dressing room, telling the kids how good they are. It's the people in town. Some of the greatest fans didn't have anybody playing. Kids need somebody to call them the night before a game, wish them luck, holler at them before a game, and hug them after a game. I mean, you pump those kids higher than a kite.

Preseason Predictions

We've been ranked No. 1 several times before the season started. I've always deemphasized the rankings. I told them, "Look, it doesn't mean anything. Whoever is ranked first, ninety-nine percent of the time is not going to win. We're going to play football, and we're going to worry about the next team we play, period. That's that." Fans are the worst ones. They'll say, "You all are so good, nobody's going to touch you until you get down to old so-and-so." That's a bunch of bull.

At the start of the season, I don't ever think we might be 6-4. I always try to figure out a way to win them all. Of course, you've got to have some common sense. When you don't have anybody, you don't have anybody. But if you get a program going like we did at Pilot Point or Celina, you're going to be decent every year. There are going to be years when you've got more talent than other years. But if you've got a program going, you can bring those kids up in it, and you'll be all right.

Questions from Parents

I've always told parents, "If you've got a question, come see me." I'll never do anything without a reason. You may not agree with the reason, but I'll explain it to you. Parents are welcome at all our practices, in the dressing room, and just about any time they want to be around. We want parents to know exactly how our program is conducted.

Moms and Dads are Different

I never had problems with daddies, but I did with mamas. A lot of women don't understand football and don't understand the price you have to pay. They think little Johnny ought to be able to miss practice and go see Grandma rather than working out. You can't do that in football season. I mean, you're committed. To me, when you commit to a team, you're committing yourself to being there every time you possibly can.

Some kids are, well, just spoiled. That's the best way I know how to say it. It's not diplomatic. I've found a lot more of that the last several years. One mom I know real well, she got up and put her boy's britches in the dryer every morning so they'd be warm when he put them on. Some of the moms would bring donuts to school between the morning workout and school instead of having them go to the lunchroom. When you're in high school, that shouldn't happen. When I was growing up, you didn't have that problem because everybody was working on the farm. Now, a lot of these mamas don't do anything but take care of those little boys.

I've got some mamas who still don't like me because we were hard on their little baby. I had a kid at Celina who was six feet, five inches and weighed about 210. He could have been a great athlete, but he quit. His mama spoiled him completely rotten. We used to box a lot in the offseason. We'd put them down on their knees right against each other with their headgear on, and they'd sit there and hit each other for twenty seconds and learn that it don't hurt to get hit.

Before we did this, I always sent a note home, saying, "This is what we're doing in the offseason. If you don't want your son to do this, we need to know." This one mama said she didn't want anybody messing with her boy, period. He was embarrassed, and all the other kids gave him a hard time. He got out of athletics. His daddy came up and met with me. He said, "I don't want to be up here. I'm up here because of my wife. The best thing that could happen to that boy is if somebody hit him right in the mouth and split his lip wide open. That's what he needs, but if you tell my wife I said that, I'm not going to admit it." He could have been a dang good football player, but his mother was so worried something was going to happen to him, she kept him scared to death all the time.

The last year I coached, I had a meeting with three mamas. Their kids were out of control and not even playing football anymore. They said, "We'd like our boys to play, but you worked them so hard that, basically, they quit." They wanted us to work them not quite as hard and let them be part of the team. I just told them, "We're going to work their tails off." They wanted me to talk to their kids, and I did. But the kids had made their decision. They didn't want to play bad enough to work.

Parents Need to Chill

Some parents, it's a wonder they don't have a heart attack – they're so wrapped up in their kids. That's not good. This is still a game. Man, I love it with a passion, but it's not as important as your family. It's not as important as your health and your church and God and things like that. That's one thing that's gotten worse over the years.

When I was playing and first started coaching, parents were working all day, and they didn't have time to be up there at school messing around. Now you've got mamas bringing their kids lunch because they don't want them to eat that old lunchroom food. That's the worst thing parents can do. That's ridiculous.

Chapter 6
<u>The Moore Magic: Teamwork Rules</u>

As soon as Moore took the job in Celina, he felt right at home.

His first stint coaching the Bobcats – from 1972 to 1976 – yielded a state championship and another deep play-off run. Now Moore prepared to get Celina back on top. Fans couldn't wait. The coach with the Midas touch had been gone for a dozen years – too long. "This could be the start of something very big – again – in Celina," the local newspaper wrote. "The enthusiasm is high, and the coach knows how to win."

Moore returned in early 1988 – just in time to start a rigorous offseason program for the players he inherited. They had played for two coaches in the previous two years, and they desperately needed direction. Under Moore, the players quickly felt a new sense of teamwork and purpose. "He taught us how to play together as a team," says Tyrone Brown, a receiver. "Before he came, everybody was pretty much playing solo. I probably learned more in that one year than I did my entire football career. Players wanted to go that extra mile for him. I loved going to workouts because it was exciting every day. With Coach Moore, the sky is the limit. There's really no comparison with those other coaches." Buster Vest, a defensive back, echoes those comments. He says Moore preached teamwork over and over. "I really didn't know what a good coach was until G.A. got hired. He hated to lose; it tore him up."

Before Moore could rebuild the Bobcats, he needed a star quarterback. He looked at the two players who had shared the position the previous season and wasn't impressed. He worked a little magic – as he had done throughout his twenty-five year coaching career. He persuaded Paul Mack, an incoming senior who hadn't played football in two years, to rejoin the team. Mack, a raw talent with a shotgun arm and blazing speed, had refused to play for the two previous coaches. "They weren't putting me in the right position," he says. "They had me on special teams, and they wanted me to play receiver or running back."

Mack knew he was a quarterback – and so did Moore. It was a huge gamble for Moore to take a rusty senior-to-be and entrust the offense to him in his pivotal first season. Moore, however, has always been a gambler. He trusted his gut, even if doubters didn't. Mack immediately bonded with the new coach and rediscovered his love of football. "Nobody had ever pushed me like G.A. did, but he did it in a good way. He stayed on me but was always encouraging. I really wish I could have played another year with G.A. He made me grow up and take care of responsibilities."

Moore addresses his Celina players before a playoff game against Holliday, 1995

Moore, who had coached a parade of quarterbacks throughout his career, saw something special in Mack – and nurtured it. "Paul Mack was smart, and he had a lot of natural ability," Moore says. "He could do things that a lot of other people couldn't do. He just got better and better and better."

In the season opener in 1988, however, Mack and the rest of the team struggled. Celina fell 19-6 to arch rival Frisco. The next week, Mack found his groove, leading the Bobcats to a 45-0 blowout of Gunter. The third game, against Pilot Point, attracted widespread attention and figured to be a stiff test. Pilot Point hadn't lost a home game in more than a decade. In the first half, the defenses prevailed, and neither team scored. In the second half, however, Celina exploded for five touchdowns to win 33-7. Mack, developing into a star, ran for two touchdowns and threw for a third. No one, not even Moore, expected Celina to dominate as it did. "I was a little surprised at the score. We got a lot of breaks, but we played hard." One local paper called it "an astonishing upset."

The *Dallas Morning News* wrote a lengthy profile of Moore afterwards, examining his legacy of success everywhere he coached. Moore is "part psychologist, part politician and one hundred percent winner," the article said. "He's devoted to the job of putting together winning football programs, and when he's been in a town that has shared his undivided attention toward that goal, the results have been stunning."

After the stirring Pilot Point victory, Celina never let up. It won its final seven games, outscoring opponents 258-37 to claim the district title. Among the routs: 57-6 over Van Alsytne and 53-7 over Pottsboro. "I think we shocked the world," Moore says recalling the 1988 season.

In the playoffs, Celina began with a 42-36 cliffhanger over Royse City. Three more wins followed: 48-18 over Olney,

38-26 over Lorena, and 29-25 over McGregor. In the latter, Celina trailed 25-22 with only four minutes remaining before Vest recovered a fumble to give the Bobcats new life. Carl Jackson then scored on a twenty-three yard touchdown run to put Celina ahead, 29-25, with less than two minutes left. McGregor, however, mounted a long drive and took the ball to Celina's eight yard line with thirty-six seconds remaining. Celina's opportunistic defense then struck again, recovering a fumble to seal the victory. Defensive tackle Terry Hendrix, who came up with the ball, says the Bobcats remained confident, even with McGregor driving late. "Determination was the key to winning this game," he told a local newspaper.

The come-from-behind victory put Celina in the semi-final game – one step from the state championship. The Bobcats would face Quanah, which had a star running back named Setrick Dickens. The week before the Celina game, Dickens rushed for 305 yards and scored all six of his team's touchdowns. Against Celina, Dickens opened the scoring with a twenty-three yard touchdown run only two minutes into the game. His backfield mate, Bubba Shaw, then scampered thirty-five yards for a touchdown to give Quanah a 14-0 first quarter lead.

Celina could never catch up. It tried mightily, twice pulling within just a touchdown, but Quanah prevailed, 42-28. The Bobcat defense, almost impenetrable all season, allowed Dickens to rush for 151 yards and two touchdowns. "He's an awfully good ballplayer," Moore said afterward. "We'd get ourselves back into the ballgame, and Quanah would make another big play. It wasn't a lack of effort. We played hard."

***

After Moore's phenomenal first year back at Celina, his legend grew even greater. A few families moved to Celina so their sons could play for Moore. Whispers of illegal recruiting intensified. Was Moore building his dynasty by raiding opposing teams? The University Interscholastic League, which governs Texas high school sports, investigated some of the complaints but never ruled against Moore. "I never recruited any of them. It's the coaches on other teams that started it. You beat them, and all of a sudden they say you recruited players. That's not right. They need to worry about their own team. I got beat by some teams, but I never accused them of recruiting."

One of the first players who moved to Celina during Moore's second stint was Terry Brockett, a quarterback from Aubrey, fifteen miles west of Celina. His father, Marion Brockett, played on Moore's first Pilot Point team in 1963. The elder Brockett had the utmost respect for the coach and wanted his son to benefit from his influence too. "I've seen him help many kids over the years," Marion Brockett says. "He's a great coach, but he's also a great man." Terry arrived in Celina as a skinny freshman, tipping the scales at only 125 pounds. He didn't appear to be a prized prospect. He played on the junior varsity his first year and then became the starting varsity quarterback as a sophomore. In three years leading the offense, Brockett had an outstanding 25-6-1 record. Moore pushed him and pushed him, turning him into one of his classic overachievers. "G.A. was hard on Terry," Marion Brockett says. "Terry would get so frustrated. I said, 'Well, he's going to make a better person out of you.'"

Terry agrees. "He could make your life miserable. You hated him while you were playing for him. It's kind of like your parents. They're really stupid until one day you wake up and realize they're not." He says Moore was a master motivator, persuading players that they could beat any team. "Our team was undersized. He demanded we work hard and give 110 percent all the time. Nothing else mattered. Effort trumped everything."

He remembers a game when Celina built a commanding 30-0 halftime lead, and players expected Moore to be pleased with their effort. Instead he found plenty to criticize. "He blew a gasket," Brockett recalls. "He said, 'You guys are not nearly as good as you think you are!' I think it was his way of not letting you relax. You were always on edge, wanting to perform your best. You didn't want to let him down." Brockett scoffs at the notion that Moore recruited him to come to Celina. "There's no way," he says. "I think I weighed 145 pounds when I was a senior. If he was going to recruit, he would have recruited someone a heck of a lot better than I was."

Like Terry's father, Alvin Evans played for Moore at Pilot Point in the 1960s. When his sons reached high school in the mid-1990s, he transferred them from Pilot Point to Celina. "I always vowed that if it was possible, my boys would play for G.A. He was a father figure – that's what I wanted. I wanted my kids in a program that taught more than football, one that taught about life – not just scoring a touchdown or making a tackle."

He ignored the talk that Moore had recruited his sons – talk that intensified after both developed into all-state linebackers. "Oh, I heard that constantly," Evans says. "There's no evidence of that whatsoever. G.A. at no times recruited us. I'd swear on a stack of Bibles."

***

G.A. Moore coached many great players during his long career. One of the best was his son, Gary Don. Born in 1977, Gary Don grew up in a home full of his father's football trophies and commemorative balls. He was the youngest of four children and the only boy. From the time he could walk, Gary Don attended football practice with his dad. "I wanted to be like him," Gary Don says. "I wanted to be with my dad and play football." He never remembers his dad teaching him about football. Instead

Gary Don simply watched practice and picked up the game's finer points. "He didn't talk much. I learned by being around him. I always knew he was special. He was demanding, but he never had to make me go to practice."

When he was in the fifth grade, Gary Don started working out with the varsity team. He'd do drills and serve as a backup quarterback, handing the ball off and throwing passes. Gary Don was a serious student of the game. His dad didn't let him practice with the big boys as a stunt. "He didn't want me to be the ball boy or towel boy. He wanted me there watching. He wanted me to learn something."

Gary Don, the tallest kid in his grade school class, quarterbacked a pee wee team. In the sixth grade, he took his team to the championship game, dazzling onlookers with his pinpoint passing and elusive running. Gary Don had honed his game against much bigger players at varsity practice. Playing against kids his own age was easy. "I thought the world of Gary Don," says John Toole, his pee wee coach. "He didn't know when to quit. He was a hustler, a leader."

G.A. had started the pee wee football program when he returned to Celina in 1988. He made sure the volunteer coaches ran the same offense and defense as the varsity. Other towns had pee wee football teams, but none were overseen by a legendary high school coach. Moore saw the pee wee team as a developmental arm of the varsity. He had the foresight to develop players long before they ever put on a Celina Bobcats jersey. Tim Looper, who played for Moore at Pilot Point in the early 1980s, served as pee wee coach in Celina. He says Moore would intently watch the youth practices and games, looking for players who could help him years down the road. "G.A. was always interested," Looper says. "He'd ask me how things were going and tell me how good a job I was doing. I tried to do my part and help out. He was my mentor. What he did inspired me. I wanted to coach like him."

In the seventh grade, Gary Don quarterbacked the Celina junior high team. In the eighth grade, however, he missed the entire season after suffering a badly broken leg in a 4-wheeler accident near his parents' ranch. The injury required surgery, and one doctor said he'd never play sports again. Another, however, was more optimistic. That doctor was Howard Moore, a family friend who served as the volunteer physician for the Celina football team. He was no relation to G.A., but he and G.A. were almost like brothers. Dr. Moore outlined an intense rehab regimen for Gary Don to try to get him ready for his freshman season. Gary Don followed it, enduring the pain without complaint. "Gary Don worked his tail off," his dad says. "He's tough."

Gary Don made the varsity as a freshman in 1992, starting as backup quarterback. He quickly became the starter when the team lost its second game. G.A. moved the

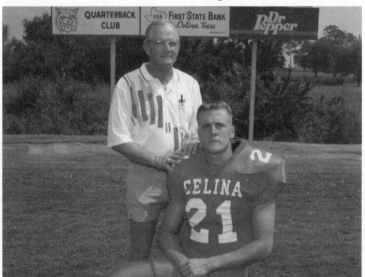

Moore with son, Gary Don as a senior, who was starting quarterback for four years, 1995

senior who had been starting to running back and elevated Gary Don. Both G.A. and Gary Don faced heavy pressure. Was G.A. starting him only because he was his son? Could Gary Don, at such a young age, command the respect of his teammates and execute the offense? G.A.'s high-risk move paid immediate dividends. In his first game as starter, Gary Don led the Bobcats to a 21-0 victory over rival Frisco. Another low-scoring game, 16-0 over Fort Worth Christian, followed. Then Gary Don and the offense kicked into high gear, routing five consecutive opponents – 63-6, 50-0, 56-6, 37-0, and 49-0 – to capture the district championship.

In the playoffs, G.A. expected the team to continue its impressive roll. Instead the Bobcats fell flat in the first game, losing 58-21 to Van Alstyne. The opponents scored three first-quarter touchdowns to pull away early. Gary Don had a forgettable night, completing only six of sixteen passes and throwing an interception. Despite the loss, G.A. remained upbeat about the season. "The kids came a long way this year," he said after the game. "I don't think anybody expected us to be very good except us."

In 1993, Gary Don returned as the starting quarterback. The season began well with a 15-8 victory over Nocona. However, a disheartening 21-14 loss to Bells followed. The Bobcats then won six straight games and seemed headed for another district title. Defeats in the final two games, however, kept Celina out of the playoffs. The offense had taken a step backward during Gary Don's sophomore season. The team averaged about twenty-four points per game, compared with thirty-five in the games he started as a freshman.

In 1994, Celina had high hopes. Gary Don would be entering his third season as a starter. His dad sometimes rode him hard, making sure he didn't grow complacent. "Anybody who was ever around practice knew he didn't baby me," Gary Don says. "I can remember other coaches feeling sorry for me a couple of times." He says that his dad, driving home from church one night, apologized to him for being too demanding. G.A. told him softly that he loved him and simply wanted him to be his best. "I knew that," Gary Don says. "I loved him too."

He and his teammates got off to a strong start in 1994. They opened with victories of 14-0 over Era and 14-6 over Little Elm. Celina's offense then exploded, winning by scores of 61-7, 62-0, and 60-0. In the final regular season game, Celina defeated arch rival Pilot Point, 21-8, to finish a perfect 10-0 and claim the district title. In the first play-off game, Celina smashed Tom Bean, 35-6. The season, however, ended the next week with a 42-6 loss to powerful Archer City. "They were the best team in the state," Gary Don says. "I got knocked out for the first time. I came back but couldn't remember any of the plays, so I ran a quarterback sneak a couple of times. Then my memory started coming back." He finished the season with impressive stats, passing for 1,461 yards and fourteen touchdowns and rushing for 859 yards and twelve scores.

When Gary Don was a senior in 1995, expectations were higher than ever. Celina fans, and even Coach Moore, talked openly of a state championship. "I don't think we would be satisfied with anything less," Moore told the local paper before the season. "It's very seldom that you get a quarterback who has had as much experience as Gary Don has." In the first game, Celina shut out Era, 49-0. Gary Don scored two rushing touchdowns. Eight blowout victories followed, with Celina scoring a total of 413 points, while allowing only forty-three. In the season's final regular season game, Celina lost to Pilot Point, 13-9. In previous years, a single district loss could cost a team the district championship, but the rules had been changed to allow two teams from each district to advance to the playoffs. Celina finished second but made the postseason along with Pilot Point.

To open the playoffs, Celina blew out Whitewright, 31-7. Gary Don rushed for ninety-five yards and three touchdowns. Two more impressive wins followed: 49-22 over Holliday and 44-6 over Rosebud-Lott. In the latter, Gary rushed for 161 yards and two touchdowns, including a seventy-four yarder. Celina then met Goldwaithe, the two-time defending state champ, in the quarterfinal game and won in a rout, 34-0. Gary Don scored three touchdowns. He also provided heroics in the next game. Celina edged West Texas, 23-22, thanks to a late sixty yard punt return for a TD by Gary Don.

The heart-stopping win put Celina in the state championship game against undefeated Alto, ranked No. 1 in the state. For the first time all season, Celina was the underdog. Alto seemed to have the clear edge in talent and depth, but Celina built a 19-14 halftime lead and held on to win 32-28. Gary Don and running back Jarrod Martin led the team to victory. Gary Don suffered a painful strained knee ligament during the game that left him limping, but he rejected calls to come out of the game. "Gary Don is one tough kid," assistant coach Danny David said afterward. "All I can say is, he was a man on a mission."

Father and son had accomplished a goal that was years in the making: a state championship. "I can remember rolling around on the field and crying, then hugging my dad and all the other coaches," Gary Don says. The game served as the crowning achievement in his playing career. For his dad, even greater accomplishments would lie ahead.

***

G.A. faced the 1996 season without the best quarterback he'd ever coached. He wasn't one to fret, though. Year after year, he took whatever talent he had and molded it into a championship-caliber team. The first season without Gary Don would be no exception.

Celina raced to a 5-0 start. The wins included routs of 61-0 over S&S and 55-0 over Paradise, relying on typical Celina smash mouth football. In the second half of the season, the Bobcats were equally as impressive, reeling off five more victories. An undefeated regular season, with less talent than the previous year, had seemed unlikely, but Moore again defied expectations. In the playoffs, the Bobcats started strong, flattening Whitewright, 47-0 and amassing 472 yards of offense. Could a second straight state championship be in the offing? In the second postseason game, Celina fell to Italy, 17-0 – a shocking end to the season. The Bobcats hadn't been held scoreless in almost a decade. "Nothing seemed to work," Moore told the local paper. "We just got beat tonight. There's not a whole lot else to say."

In 1997, Moore began his pursuit of another state championship – just as he did every fall. This season, however, began in abysmal fashion. Celina dropped the opener, 21-7 to Denton Liberty, and the second game, 35-34 to Sanger. In almost thirty-five years of coaching, Moore had lost the first two games of a season only once before – way back in 1967 at Pilot Point. How would this Celina bunch respond to the early adversity? The Bobcats reeled off eight straight victories to earn a playoff spot. They were peaking at the perfect time.

In the first postseason game, Celina demolished Bells, 59-6. The Bobcats built a 46-6 halftime lead and never let up. "Our defense just played real well, and our special teams played as well as they have in a long time," Moore says. In the next game, Celina needed a dramatic finish to win the game. Celina and Mart were tied 15-15, with three minutes and fifteen seconds left. The Bobcats marched eighty-six yards in eight plays, scoring the winning touchdown with less than a minute remaining. "The kids got together before that last drive and decided if we were going to get where we wanted to get, we were going to have to score," Moore said afterward. "They just got after it."

Celina had less trouble the next week, defeating Holliday 20-7. The Bobcats scored first and never trailed. The victory set up a rematch against Italy, the team that ended Celina's season the year before with a rare shutout. This time, the Bobcats scored, but they didn't score enough. Italy won, 28-20. "They came up with the big plays and capitalized," Moore says. "That was the difference in the game." Despite the loss, Celina enjoyed a remarkable season – making a deep playoff run after a 0-2 start. Moore was in his coaching prime, or so it seemed. He'd won four state championships, dating back to 1974, and contended for several more. Starting in 1998, however, his legend grew ever greater.

***

The next level of Moore's career began with a 54-0 blowout of Aubrey midway through the 1998 season. It marked the start of a state record fifty-seven game winning streak by Celina. During the run, the Bobcats won four straight

Celina players and coaches celebrating fourth straight state championship, 2001. Photo courtesy of Fred Helms

state championships to tie a state record. After winning the title in 1998 with a 14-2 record, Celina didn't lose a game in 1999, 2000, or 2001. Each season, the Bobcats finished a perfect 16-0, ending the season with a championship trophy. Moore and Celina became known around the country for football dominance.

Moore had developed a foolproof formula for winning, and one of the key ingredients was attention to detail. For instance, his playbook emphasized the importance of the kicking game. "Good teams have good kicking games!!!" he wrote. "Details such as proper technique, knowledge of kicking rules, and avoiding foolish penalties are very important. You must have poise and confidence in yourself and the team, which no set of circumstances can change. Must be consistent. Do it right every time! Must have a high degree of intensity. Must be TOUGH. There is absolutely no room for the weak and faint of heart on the kicking teams."

In 2001, *USA Today* published a big spread on the coach and the team. The writer asked Moore how he could be so successful year after year. "We don't have the size and number to choose from like a 5A school, but it still boils down to blocking and tackling, and we do that as well as anybody," he said. Moore taught his players to master the fundamentals. Occasionally, he'd run a trick play, but nothing pleased him more than dominating the other team at the line of scrimmage. On offense, that meant blowing the defensive players off the ball and running for daylight. On defense, it meant neutralizing the blockers and crushing the ball carrier.

Shortly after the *USA Today* article, *Texas Monthly* profiled Moore and examined his success. The article emphasized Moore's focus on the fundamentals. "G.A. Moore . . . exudes all the flash and sparkle of a dirt farmer," it began. The writer asked Moore his secret. "What it comes down to, I guess, is I just don't like to get beat."

Even as his success grew, his ego never did. Moore always preferred to give others credit. When the team won, the players executed well, he would say. When it lost, he failed to prepare them adequately. In the 2001 season, Celina won its fiftieth consecutive game to break a state record that had stood since 1957. During the extensive newspaper coverage, Moore never blew his own horn. "I've been so blessed," he told the *Dallas Morning News*. "The good Lord has let this take place. I don't know why...It humbles you when you really stop and think about it."

In the playoffs, Celina rolled over five opponents to reach the state title game. The Bobcats faced Garrison in a game that became an instant classic. Celina won, 41-35, but not without a monumental struggle. Garrison led 35-27 in the third quarter, thanks to a powerful running back who scored four touchdowns. Celina's normally stout defense kept surrendering big plays. "For the first time in my career, I thought we might lose," says Brian Babbitt, a Celina guard.

Moore knew the team needed a spark. He pulled aside Ryan Conner, an undersized but ferocious middle linebacker. "He put his arm around me and looked me straight in the face," Conner recalls. "He says, 'If we're going to win, do something.'" Conner's improvised response: do a "front" in the middle of the field, before his teammates, opponents, and spectators. For years, Moore had made his players do "fronts" at practice to toughen them up. Players lined up side by side and leaped forward at an angle, their arms behind their backs, hitting the ground with a loud and painful thud. Players dreaded fronts.

With the championship game against Garrison slipping away, Conner decided a front would be a show of resolve that could inspire his teammates and intimidate the opponent. He took a few steps out of the defensive huddle and, summoning all his might, propelled himself as high and as far as he could, locking his sweaty hands behind his grimy jersey. Conner felt pain, naturally, when he hit the ground, but he also had a surge of adrenalin that wiped out the pain and filled him with strength. "I made the next tackle and got pretty jacked up. The defensive line then stepped up and had a few sacks. I could see something in their faces. From then on, we stepped up to a whole new level."

Shortly after the front, Celina scored on a twenty-two yard run late in the third quarter to narrow Garrison's lead to 35-33. In the fourth quarter, Celina's defense dug deep and held the powerful Garrison offense to only twelve yards of offense. The momentum had shifted. The Bobcat offense, inspired by the defense's turnaround, took care of business, marching down the field to score on a one yard touchdown plunge to win the game 41-35. Relief overwhelmed the Celina players. They had kept the streak of championships alive. "There was so much pressure, looking back," Conner says. "I don't think I've ever had as much pressure put on me, in work or in family, since then. We treated it almost like a profession. It's tough when the bar is so high. You go 16-0 and win state; otherwise, it's a failure."

Conner, Babbitt, quarterback Jordan Martin, and safety Nik Prosser played on all four of the championship teams from 1998-2001. They have similar accounts of how Moore kept the players motivated and pushed them both psychologically and physically to achieve greatness. "He never let us get too high or too low," Conner says. "If we were the best team on the field, he taught us to respect our opponent enough not to have any slipups. If we weren't the favorite, he always got our minds ready to play. He ingrained mental toughness in us."

Babbitt agrees. "We never felt intimidated. We were ready to kick butt and take names. You wanted to keep that streak going." Players bought into Moore's concept of team first, individual second, Prosser says. "You wanted to sell out for him and the team. He found a way to get everybody to perform at their highest level. He invested in each person. He wanted you to know the team was counting on you. You understood your role, and it meant something."

Prosser has several photos of himself and Moore on the sidelines, the coach's arm draped around his shoulder. "You knew he always had your back," Prosser says. "He consistently got you to perform above what you thought you could. The funny thing was he never expected more than you could deliver. That made you respect him and love him."

One of Moore's biggest honors was being named to coach the North squad of the Texas High School Coaches Association All Star game in Houston after the 2001 season. Moore took with him his entire coaching staff, whom he credited for much of his success. Celina's Jordan Martin scored a late touchdown to lead the North squad to victory and put a bow on Celina's accomplishment of winning four straight state title games.

***

After Celina won its fourth championship, accolades poured in for Moore. Newspapers and magazines praised him. Former players and fellow coaches flooded him with congratulatory calls and notes. Moore also started hearing from his friends and backers in Pilot Point. Once again, the Pilot Point football program had fallen on hard times – just as it always seemed to when Moore wasn't coaching. School superintendent Cloyce Purcell, whom Moore had once hired as an assistant coach, called and asked if he could meet with Moore.

At first, Purcell said he simply wanted Moore's input on rebuilding the team. He didn't suggest that he would try to hire Moore away from Celina. Moore says he felt obligated, as a friend of Purcell's, to hear about the problems facing the Pilot Point program and offer some suggestions. Moore never expected Purcell to offer him the job. After all, Moore had the dream situation in Celina. Not only had he won fifty-seven straight games and four consecutive state titles, the future looked equally bright. Another championship – and maybe another and another – seemed within reach. Moore couldn't have asked for a more supportive community than he had in Celina. He had absolutely no reason to be discontent.

After a few meetings with Purcell, however, Moore began to wonder. His talks with the superintendent started to take a subtle turn. Purcell went from asking for Moore's advice to gauging his interest in the job. Purcell had to be patient and cautious, like an angler trying to land a prized catch. Moore tried to keep the meetings with Purcell a secret. In small towns, however, secrets are hard to keep. Soon Celina insiders found out that Pilot Point again was courting Moore. Love triangles eventually lead to hurt feelings. Such was the case when Moore confounded and angered many Celina fans by accepting the Pilot Point job in early 2002.

Moore called it the most difficult decision of his life – by far. At the time, he didn't elaborate on his reasons for leaving Celina. Aware of the hurt feelings and conflicted about the move, Moore says he retreated internally. Now, years later, he's willing to talk about his decision. He says he felt God pulling him back to Pilot Point. Moore, a Baptist deacon and Sunday school teacher who once quit coaching to consider the ministry, cared more about what God thought than what people thought, more about his spiritual life than his coaching life.

"I got to feeling awkward in Celina because they treated me like a king," Moore says. "We'd won four straight championships, and I felt like I was getting too much credit. My wife and I pray all the time, and we prayed the

Lord would humble us. I think this was his way of humbling me because I was in the greatest situation there ever was."

Moore got humbled – right off the bat. Several Celina players who would be seniors the next fall felt betrayed. They thought Moore had promised to come back to seek a fifth straight title. They viewed Moore as a trusted father who had suddenly abandoned the family. Moore says he understood their dismay. "I had no intention of going to Pilot Point *at all*," he says. "When I resigned, I couldn't even talk to the kids. I did not want to leave Celina because I loved that place. I just felt like I was doing what I was supposed to do."

Gradually Celina players and fans accepted Moore's decision, even if they didn't understand it. The new Celina coach would be a familiar figure. Butch Ford had been Moore's top assistant for twenty-five years – covering stints in Pilot Point, Sherman, and Celina. Ford had also played for Moore at Pilot Point in the late 1960s. Succeeding the fatherly Moore at Celina was bittersweet for Ford. He wanted a chance, finally, to be a head coach, but he didn't want to disrupt the winning formula he and Moore had developed. Ford tried to persuade Moore to stay, but his mind was set. "We split on good terms," Ford says.

Ford had plenty of talent on his Celina team, and players quickly rallied around him. They missed Moore, but Ford had a Moore-like ability to get players to focus and play their hardest. The Bobcats won their first six games, extending the school's state-record winning streak to sixty-three games. The seventh game would be an emotional one when Celina faced Pilot Point. The legendary coach versus the pupil. The greatest 3A team in the state versus a rebuilding one. The wounds over Moore's move to Pilot Point would be reopened with the critical matchup. "The stress of that game was unbelievable," Ford says. "It was a very unpleasant experience. I hated it, and he hated it."

Moore agrees. "It wasn't any fun."

The game was played in Pilot Point on a stormy night. Heavy rain turned the field into a mud pit, and the sloppy conditions hampered the offenses. Celina won, 10-0. When the game ended, an eerie silence filled the stadium. Celina players and coaches didn't feel like celebrating. They were almost embarrassed to defeat Moore. It was as if they had kicked their grandfather in the shins. Moore and Ford met in the middle of the field afterward and hugged. Their exchange was captured by a film crew documenting Ford's first year as head coach.

"That was the hardest game I ever spent," Moore told Ford.

"I didn't enjoy it either," Ford replied. "Thanks for all you did for me."

Both teams won the rest of their regular season games to make the playoffs. Celina finished first in district, Pilot Point second. In the playoffs, both teams bowed out early. Pilot Point lost its first game, while Celina fell in its second. The winning streak, which Moore had started and built to fifty-seven games, ended at sixty-eight under Ford. Would Celina have won a fifth straight state championship if Moore had stayed? No one knows.

In the next two seasons, Celina and Pilot Point met again. Celina won twice more, 17-6 and 27-21. Ford felt no pride in beating the master, and Moore felt no shame in losing to Celina. He still believed he had obeyed God's will in going to Pilot Point, and he had revived the program. In three seasons, Moore compiled a 22-12 record and made the playoffs each season. More importantly, Moore had shaped young men's lives. Jarail Johnson serves as an example. By his own admission, Johnson had been a troublemaker at school before Moore arrived. He quit the football team and had run-ins with teachers. Under Moore, however, Johnson rekindled his love of football and settled down emotionally. "G.A. Moore had a lot of influence on me. He was one of those people who inspired me to try to live a cleaner life, make better decisions, and put faith in God. He really took me under his wing. A lot of people look at G.A. Moore as a football coach. He's more than a football coach – he's a powerful leader."

Moore resigned from Pilot Point after the 2004 season. Health problems forced his hand. He had grown increasingly fatigued, unable to work the marathon hours as he had throughout his career. "I didn't have the energy to get involved in the community, to do the things I'd always done. I came to the conclusion I was getting old." A medical exam revealed he had a severely clogged artery, and heart surgery ensued. Moore gradually recovered, "piddling" with his cattle until the coaching bug bit him again.

In 2009, five years after leaving coaching, Moore took the head job at Aubrey, less than a half-hour's drive from both Pilot Point and Celina. Unlike those towns, however, Aubrey had no history of football excellence. Moore's job was to establish a winning tradition, and he succeeded immediately. In his first season, Aubrey started 5-0, outscoring opponents 204-0. At age seventy-one, Moore had built perhaps his finest defense ever. "Once we started winning, it was just surreal," says Levi Birdsong, a receiver. "He taught us that the football team was a family, and you'd do anything to save your brother. We'd push ourselves harder and harder, thinking the guy next to me is fighting for me, and I've got to fight for him."

In the second half of the regular season, Aubrey continued its dominance and earned a playoff spot. The Chaparrals blasted their first two postseason opponents 34-7 and 27-7 before falling to McGregor 31-21. Aubrey had finished an unexpected 11-2, and Moore had created football fever in a town that never experienced it. "He exceeded all expectations," says former superintendent James

Monaco. "There were more people at practices, more people at games. When I hired him, I said, 'G.A., I want you to work your magic here. I just want to be part of that magic.'"

Moore spent two more seasons in Aubrey before retiring, but they were disappointing ones. Moore suffered the only losing records in his forty-five year coaching career, going 4-6 in both 2010 and 2011. The records were understandable, considering that Aubrey's growing enrollment nudged it into a higher classification with much larger schools. Moore hated to lose, as always, but the uncharacteristic defeats didn't torment him. "Not under the circumstances," he says. "If it had been thirty years ago, it would have eaten on me."

Steve Scribner had two sons play for Moore during his tenure at Aubrey. "I couldn't have been more excited. He changed the whole mentality. He had a way of making a kid want to give 110 percent on Friday night or even at practice. I spent a lot of time talking to him, and I never heard him say anything bad about a kid. I never saw him get in a kid's face and humiliate him. The kids respected him."

Scribner wonders if Moore might come out of retirement again and resume coaching somewhere. Others have expressed the same thought. "I saw him the other day, and he still looks pretty dadgum good," Scribner says. "I think he's got something inside of him that burns. A lot of people say, 'Here's a man who really loves football.' I think that's true, but I'd say, 'Here's a guy who really loves kids.'"

In His Own Words...My Playing Career

I Made My Daddy Proud

My mother didn't want me to play football. She was afraid I was going to get hurt. She had a brother who was a good football player, but he got bunged up. He was a hoss. I was only four or five years old, but I'd go down to the football field and watch them practice every day. He was a running back. They had those old leather helmets. He always talked to me about football. He got me interested in playing ball.

My dad never did play football, but he backed me. He talked to my mother, and I got to play. I never will forget my first game. It was against Muenster my freshman year. I went out behind the school before the game and prayed, "Lord, just help me not to be scared." I intercepted two passes – that was a big deal to me. Daddy came up to me and said, "I was so proud of the way you played." That was one of the highlights of my life – my first football game.

Opening Up the Gym

When I was in high school and we had a big ballgame, they'd open up the gym afterward. Our dressing room was underneath the gym. We'd come out, and all the people in town would be out there in the gym. They'd get the drink machines open. A lot of times, they'd go get a bunch of cookies. The superintendent and principal didn't have no choice. The people in town said, "This is our school, and we're going to do this."

It wasn't just the mamas and daddies of players. It was all the people in town. I was raised like that. When we played, we always had more fans than the other team. It didn't matter what sport it was – we always had such great support from the town. I learned you need that support. No coach can go in and do things by himself. He's got to have support from the administration, the school board, the teachers, and the community. The teams I coached weren't always the best, but we had the right attitude and the support of everybody.

Facemasks

We didn't have facemasks when I first started playing high school football. From the first practice until the end of the season, we never had any skin on our nose. It was always getting skinned off from hitting the ground. We had scabs, and we'd pick them off when a game started and mash it and wipe the blood around your face – just to make you look mean. Before my senior year, we finally got facemasks. It was at the end of a weeklong training camp where we stayed at the school. The facemasks came in on a Saturday morning, and the coach told us, "If you want to get it put on, you can stay up here. If you don't, go on home with your folks." Anyway, I came on home. All my relatives were out there.

That night, we played Whitesboro in a scrimmage, and a guy came over a pile with his knee and caved my cheekbone in. If I'd had a facemask on, it probably wouldn't have happened. They wound up carrying me to Denton and then to Dallas to have surgery. They went through my mouth and up behind my ear and wired my cheekbone together. They cut the nerves, and I don't have any feeling on that side of my face. Stupidly, I came back and played five weeks later. They bought me a facemask like they use now – like linemen wear. Nobody else had one.

Wichita Falls

My sophomore year at Pilot Point, we went to the play-offs. They closed down the town and took a train to Wichita Falls for the game. I mean, everybody in town went. Those people didn't have any money. Everybody was farmers. But they had enough money to support us, and we knew it. We all knew we had more support than anybody in the country.

This was probably wrong, but back then people used to give me milk shakes. Those old farmers would come up and put their arm around you and tell you how proud they were of you. They'd say, "Hey, come in here, let's get something to eat." They'd pay for it. They were taking care of us because they cared for us as a person. It wasn't because we were a great athlete.

The guys that were doing that didn't have any kids playing. That's just the way they were. Those rascals were always going to whoop the referees if we didn't win. They backed us one hundred percent. They took off from their jobs and came down to our pep rallies in the middle of the day and talked to us about winning. We knew everybody in Pilot Point was backing us, and that made such a difference.

Injuries

I got concussions when I was playing. It wasn't a big deal. Everybody got knocked out. They'd ask you what your name was, then you'd go back in and play. Back then, they'd teach you to hit them in the ear hole – put your headgear right on his ear hole and rattle his brain. That'll get his attention, and he won't play very well. Nobody thought that was dirty. It was just football. Now they're saying that can cause brain damage. I guess it didn't to me.

In college, I thought I could hit harder than anybody else. I wasn't that big. I weighed only 170 pounds. I got bunged up because I played a little too reckless. I was stupid, really. Oh, Lord, I had my ribs caved in, my collarbone busted. One day, we were doing head-on tackling drills in practice. The coaches were mad at everybody. They said, "Who thinks they're tough enough to get out there?" Old Charlie Cole says, "G.A. does. He's from Pilot Point. He's the toughest sucker out here." I almost got killed. I wanted to tell him, "Shut up, Charlie." It was punishment back then – you knocked the fire out of each other. Nowadays, you're not supposed to hit with the helmets. They didn't have those rules back when I was playing.

Another time, I took a handoff at practice, and a linebacker hit me on the wrist and broke it. I wore a cast, and they fixed a brace with a hinge on it. I tried to come back the next fall with that brace on. I made it through four days of camp, and my wrist popped in two again. That was one of the most defining moments of my life. I woke up, and I couldn't play football anymore. I thought my life was over. All I ever went to school for was to play ball. I decided, hey man, I want to get an education. I started studying and making good grades, and I graduated. I think the Good Lord used football to get me in a position to get an education and have an opportunity to coach.

Chapter 7
<u>Winning in Football, Winning in Life</u>

Rex Glendenning weighed only 110 pounds as a freshman football player at Celina High School in the early 1970s. "I was a runt," he says. The next season, he reached only 120 pounds. He was still a runt. It wasn't until Glendenning's junior season, when he beefed up to a modest 145 pounds, when he started to look like a football player.

Glendenning eventually grew to 190 pounds as a senior, became an all-state middle linebacker, and earned a scholarship to North Texas State University, where he was a two-year starter and co-captain. He credits G.A. Moore, his Celina coach, for having faith in him as he developed into a star. "If he had cut players, I'd probably have been cut my freshman or sophomore year," Glendenning says. "There are three people I consider life changers in my life: my grandfather, father, and G.A. Moore. G.A. is a very special guy. He epitomizes winning."

Glendenning, who still lives in Celina, achieved success as a high school and college football player, but he's achieved even more success as a businessman. Today, he's a high-profile commercial real estate agent who has brokered some of the biggest land deals in the North Dallas area for the past twenty years. He's worked closely on the projects with Dallas Cowboys owner Jerry Jones, who has made his mark in real estate development as well as football.

Glendenning recently sold Jones on the idea of a ninety-one acre mixed-use development in Frisco, twenty-five miles north of Dallas, which will include a hotel, offices, shops, and a new headquarters for the Cowboys. The team is moving from another Dallas suburb, Irving. Playing for Moore, with his lofty standards, helped prepare Glendenning for the high-pressure world of multimillion dollar real estate deals, he says. "When you look Jerry Jones in the eye and say, 'This is what we need to do – move the Cowboys from Irving to Frisco, and here's how we're going to do it' – you'd better have your game face on, and you'd better be right. G.A. always kept on an even keel, through thick and thin. In pressure situations, like state games, he remained calm and methodical and figured out a way to get this done. Where there's a will, there's a way."

Although Glendenning is enjoying his greatest success now, he's known failure in business. In the 1980s, a real estate downturn left him bankrupt. "I've been broke – not near broke," he says. He applied the lessons of perseverance he learned under Moore. "There are so many reasons to quit in this business or any business. You've got to fight through it. G.A. Moore instilled in somebody a winning spirit and a never-quit attitude. If you quit, you're letting yourself down, your family down, your friends down, and your community down."

He still sees Moore occasionally and admires the influence he's had on generations of young men. "G.A. Moore wants to win football games, but I think what separates him from most high school and college coaches is that he's truly about making the student athlete a better person when he leaves the stage," Glendenning says. "I've seen G.A. through the years, whether it was in Pilot Point or Celina, get up in the morning and take kids to school. I've seen him take them home and feed them at his house. There are a lot of kids who fell through the cracks. There was poverty in both Pilot Point and Celina. He sought kids like that out. I've personally seen about thirty to forty kids that he's basically been a surrogate father to. A few had athletic ability, but the bulk didn't. I'd say there are thousands of young men who have had success in life long term because of the foundation he laid in their lives.

He embodied God, family, hard work, and ethics in the students he coached."

Moore always emphasized team success over individual achievement, Glendenning says. "G.A. didn't want one star. He didn't want one guy getting all the press. He wanted the team to get recognition and the community to shine because of it. He built unselfish players. If he thought somebody was being selfish, he would do everything within his power to teach them to be unselfish. Sometimes you weren't going to like it. He could be very tough, but you probably deserved every bit of the chewing you were getting."

Glendenning, who has dark hair and intense eyes, played on Moore's first state championship team in 1974. Then, as in later years, Celina didn't have a roster full of outstanding athletes. "When you'd see a Celina team run out on the field, you'd say, 'They're fixing to get their asses kicked.' Most of his teams didn't have speed, size, or talent. Basically, his success was by outworking his opponent. His players believed in him, and he believed in them. It was a testament to his great coaching."

Ten years ago, Glendenning gave $50,000 to his college alma mater, now called the University of North Texas, to name the coaches' office after Moore. Moore, like Glendenning, starred as a football player there. "I think so much of him. He's an honorable, real human being. So many people try to put on a facade. He doesn't. He's a good, hardworking coach who happens to be a Christian and care about the community. He walks the walk. The way he lives his life is a testament to his beliefs."

***

Butch Ford spent twenty-five years as an assistant coach under G.A. Moore. "That's longer than most people have been married," Ford says. During that time together, Ford and Moore experienced a multitude of highs and lows, just as in a marriage. Together, they won state championships in 1980 and 1981 in Pilot Point and in 1995, 1998, 1999, 2000, and 2001 in Celina. They also had a few seasons in which they missed the playoffs.

Before Ford coached with Moore, he played for him. Ford was a standout running back for Pilot Point in the mid-1960s, early in Moore's coaching career. During that time, the school integrated racially and won two district championships. Ford admired Moore's tough love approach as a coach. He had high standards for players, but he cared for them as individuals. "People have an expectation of what a coach is," Ford says. "Usually it's a hard, crusty guy who cusses you out. G.A. is different than that. Now he's got a temper, but foul language was not accepted. You felt like he loved you and cared for you as a person. You wanted to please him." When Ford became a senior, he started thinking about his career options. He decided to be a coach. "I wanted to be just like G.A. He worked the crap out of me, but I had a positive experience. We'd run through a brick wall for him. I think that's the secret to coaching – getting kids to trust you that well."

Ford was an assistant coach at Pilot Point in 1977 when Moore took over as head coach. The two developed a strong relationship as the program prospered. Ford quickly learned that Moore had high standards for his assistant coaches, just as he did for his players. Ford eventually became defensive coordinator, and he often spent hours watching film of opponents and developing game plans. Sometimes Moore would tear them up and draft his own plans. "He could make you mad," Ford says. "His expectation level was very high. We disagreed, but we'd get over it and move on. "

Ford had several chances to be a head coach while working for Moore, but he always chose to stay with his mentor. They developed a formula for success, and Ford didn't want to disrupt it. Ford accepted that he might be an assistant to Moore his entire career. In 2001, however, Moore unexpectedly stepped down as Celina coach after the team won its fourth straight state championship. In a move that confused and angered Celina supporters, Moore returned to Pilot Point for a third coaching stint. The Celina school board then offered Ford the head coaching job. He finally got his chance at age fifty, and he made the most of it.

He extended Celina's state-record fifty-seven game winning streak to sixty-eight games in his first season in 2002. That year, a documentary film producer followed Ford and his team as Celina started a new era without Moore. During halftime of a critical playoff game that was tied, Ford delivered a stirring speech – just as Moore often would. "Now is not the time to panic!" he said. "It's time to fight! Bow your neck and make up your mind you will not be defeated!" Energized, the Bobcats scored three second-half touchdowns and held the other team scoreless to win 35-21. Later, Ford took Celina to four straight state championship games from 2005 through 2008, winning two and losing two. He earned the respect of players, parents, and community members as a worthy successor to the immortal G.A. Moore.

As a gesture of his appreciation to Moore, Ford presented him with a commemorative football with their awe-inspiring joint coaching record inscribed on it. It was 277-38-4. Ford, who has a square jaw, thick gray hair, and a gentle manner, retired in 2012 after a decade as Celina coach. He lives on fifty-seven acres outside of town and has an office full of trophies, game balls, photographs, and memorabilia from his successful coaching career. It wouldn't have been possible without the influence of Moore. "I owe him everything," Ford says. "Without a doubt, I wouldn't be coaching if it wasn't for him. He created an atmosphere in the community that we're going to win. Most places don't have that. Celina is still proud of that. I felt we won a ton of games we shouldn't have because our kids thought they were going to win."

***

After Ford retired as Celina coach, he was replaced by another G.A. Moore devotee: Bill Elliott. Like Ford, Elliott played for Moore and coached with him. Elliott was a standout lineman at Pilot Point in the mid-1980s and, after a stellar career at TCU, joined Moore on the staff at Celina in 1992. "I knew in high school I wanted to be a coach," Elliott says. "I had a great relationship with Coach Moore. When you first started playing for him, you're almost mesmerized. There was an aspect of fear because he was G.A. Moore. But as you got to know him, you understood how much he cared about kids. We practiced with intensity. He taught us to give everything we had on every play – to leave it all on the field. He pushed me to be the best athlete I could be."

Elliott coached alongside Moore as Celina won five state championships from 1995 to 2001. He studied Moore's methods and applied them when he became the Bobcats' head coach. "G.A. was the master at getting the best out of his kids. Every kid is different. Some coaches are just *rah-rah-rah, drive-drive-drive* all the time. Some kids respond to that, and some don't. G.A. figured out a way to reach each kid. He knew their abilities and how to motivate them – whether it was getting after them or patting them on the back. He got kids to buy into what he was teaching."

Elliott had immediate success when he took over the storied Celina program. He advanced to the playoffs in each of his first three seasons and in 2015 made it to the championship game. Before the game, televised live, Elliott tried to motivate the team by invoking the school's proud heritage. "You are the Celina Bobcats!" he told the players in the locker room. "You're the big dog in Texas football. All the tradition. All the legacy. Get it done!"

Unfortunately, in the highly anticipated game, Celina's quarterback suffered a broken arm early, and his inexperienced replacement struggled. Celina fell 22-3 to West Orange-Stark. Losing the quarterback "pretty much blew our chances," Elliott says. "He was such a huge part of our offense."

After the game, Elliott tried to comfort his distraught players. "Everything happens for a reason," he says. "That's how I view life, and that's what Coach Moore taught me. We didn't win, but life goes on. You have to pick yourself up and go on and fight the next challenge. We're going to have battles we deal with in our family, in our job, that are going to be bigger and more important than that game."

Like Moore, Elliott believes his job description involves more than winning championships. "I'm here to win, and I want to win bad, but I really feel like I'm here to try to make these boys into men. My job is to teach them how to grow up to be husbands and fathers and people in our community. I think that's the biggest problem we have in our society today: Too many kids aren't being taught by their dad how to be a real man. Coach Moore always said coaching is a calling, almost like being a preacher. I feel God has called me to be a coach to teach these boys what it is to be a man."

Elliott, who stands six feet and five inches and still lifts weights regularly, once dreamed of being a professional football player. He was offered a free agent contract by the Chicago Bears, but he tore up a knee while filming a movie. He was an extra in a film called *Necessary Roughness*. "It was stupid," Elliott laughs. "I tried to be a movie star." People sometimes ask if he regrets missing out on the NFL. "A lot of kids go, 'Man, don't you wish you could have played?' Even my own boys ask me because they'll watch my old videos. If it had worked out, I wouldn't be here, and I wouldn't have gotten to do all the things I've done in Celina. I wouldn't have had the influence I've had on kids' lives. I think it was God's way of closing one door and opening another and directing me to where I needed to go. I'm perfectly content here."

Like Ford, Elliott credits Moore for shaping his career. "I love Coach Moore. He's done so many great things for me. When I see him, we talk and hug and share. I'd still do anything in the world for him."

*****

Moore inspired scores of other players during his forty-five year career to enter coaching. Some, such as Elliott and Ford, stayed in Celina and kept the Moore mojo going. Others, such as Danny David, replicated Moore's formula for success at other schools. David played under Moore at Pilot Point, winning state titles in 1980 and 1981. He then coached under Moore at Celina and Pilot Point from 1990 to 2004, winning five championships.

In 2005, David got his chance to be a head coach at Collinsville, a smaller town twenty miles north of Celina. He took a downtrodden program and built it into a perennial winner. In his eleven years there, the team has made the playoffs eight times. He patterns his coaching philosophy – the way he calls plays and the way he treats players – after Moore.

"Everything we do is based on what he taught," David says. "He wasn't the type of coach to grab your facemask. He wasn't degrading. He'd get onto you, but he'd never let you leave the field house unhappy. He's like a second father to me. He's why I do what I do today, because of the influence he had on me as a player and as a coach. I saw the way he gave back to the kids and the community. I thought that was something I would like to do. He had the unique ability to take average kids and get them to play above average. We never had the best athletes, but a lot of times we had the best teams. It was the work ethic he instilled in us. We believed we could outwork people."

Like Elliott, David is still looking for his first state title. But he notes that Moore's primary goal was always to turn out winning kids, not produce championship teams. "You can't be a champion on the field and a turd in the school hallway. It's about turning out kids that will be a positive part of society. That's when you know if you've got a winning program. It's not winning state championships. It's about teaching and the relationships you develop with these kids."

***

Junior Worthey also played for Moore, but he never went into coaching. Instead, he was influenced by the legendary coach in a much different way. Because of Moore, Worthey has a son he wouldn't have otherwise.

One day in late 1997 Moore called Worthey and his wife, Verna, and asked if they would consider taking in a troubled teen named Keylan Basham. Keylan had an abysmal home life. He hadn't lived with his parents for two years because they had been in and out of prison on drug and theft charges. Keylan stayed with first one friend, then another, before he wore out his welcome. Moore had coached Keylan's older brother Clint several years earlier in Celina, and he knew that Keylan was basically a good kid who had been dealt a bad hand of cards.

Moore thought the Wortheys – regular churchgoers who had already raised three sons – could provide the discipline and stability that Keylan needed. Junior and Verna said they would consider opening their home to Keylan, who was a freshman, but they wanted to meet him first. So one Friday afternoon, Moore brought Keylan to the Worthey's home. Keylan shook their hands awkwardly. "I was scared," he recalls.

Worthey, a towering standout lineman for Moore at Pilot Point in the 1960s, initially intimidated Keylan. He made it clear he had non-negotiable rules: Keylan would be home at 10 p.m. on weekdays and midnight on weekends – not a minute later. He would go to church every Sunday. He would improve his grades. And, most of all, he would respect and obey Verna. Junior worked long hours at a truck assembly plant, and Verna often would be the only parent in the house. "I said, 'If you're not willing to do what she says, I would suggest you not even think about staying at this house,'" Junior recalls.

Keylan nodded his head in agreement to each of the conditions, relieved that he might finally have a home. Quickly, Keylan started calling the Wortheys "Mom" and "Dad," and his life began to take shape. He enjoyed going to church, and he began to take school seriously. The next year, as a sophomore, Keylan made the Celina varsity football team coached by Moore. By mid-season, Keylan had become a starting linebacker. The team won the state championship that year – as well as the next two years. The Wortheys attended every game and cheered him on – just as they had their biological son, Ryan, who played on another of Moore's championship teams in 1995.

Junior and Verna never legally adopted Keylan, but it didn't make any difference. Keylan was their son. They knew it, and he knew it. "There's a lifelong bond," Keylan says. "It's never going to change." Almost twenty years after moving in with the Wortheys, Keylan attends all the family functions and drops by to see Mom and Dad on a regular basis. Pictures of his wife and daughter are displayed alongside pictures of their other kids and grandkids. "Love is love," says Keylan, now a construction superintendent. "Even today, if something happens or I'm having a difficult time, I can ask them whatever I want to ask them."

He's grateful to the Wortheys and to G.A. Moore. "Words cannot express what kind of guy he is and what he's done for me. I didn't realize until later in life, looking back, what that little phone call [to the Wortheys] did for me. There's no doubt in my mind – with my family's history – that if G.A. had not made that phone call, I would not be married or have a job. I'd probably be in prison."

And, without Moore's intervention, Junior and Verna wouldn't have another son. "We treated him just like one of ours," Verna says. "To this day, he thanks us for taking him in. He'll tell us, 'I don't know what I'd have been if you hadn't.'"

***

Moore influenced countless others during his decades of coaching. Many took the time to write Moore heartfelt letters of appreciation and admiration. He cherished and kept each one. In 1995, the mother of a player wrote to the Celina principal, saying she was impressed that Moore had the players visit a nursing home only days before a critical playoff game. "This type of leadership is one of the many reasons we wanted Jarrod to come to Celina," wrote Carol Martin. "It is obvious to this mom that Coach Moore and his assistants teach our kids more than just the plays of the week. Thanks for leadership that reinforces what we, as parents, teach our kids – respect, a caring attitude, showing value for people. These young people will emerge as winners in life – and these fine coaches certainly should be thanked."

Another mom, Catalina Maddox, wrote Moore four years later. Her husband had recently died after a long battle with cancer. Their son was a senior on the football team, and Moore became a "father and friend" to him, she wrote. "I want to tell you that without your support, I would not have known what to do with Frank Jr. My debt to you is enormous…What you do for these children in one day is beyond anything I or anyone else could do in a lifetime. Building confidence, teaching self-respect, keeping young people out of trouble, giving them the chance to dream and making dreams come true are gifts that can only come from great wise souls. I will always remember the important role you played in my son's life, and I know that he will never forget you either. I also know that my beloved husband is thanking you for what you did for his son. He knew that his only son was in great hands. He died in peace because of that."

Her son, Frank Maddox Jr., recalls that his dad's funeral was held on a Saturday after a football game the previous night. Moore cancelled practice so all the players could attend the funeral. "He was very, very comforting," Maddox says. "After my father passed, he was like a father figure to me. He was one of the people I turned to whenever I needed advice or help with anything. I could always go to him. No coach has ever come close to having that kind of influence on my life."

Guy Charles, who played on the same team as Maddox, wrote Moore's son, Gary Don, a letter praising his dad. "I moved to Celina the beginning of my freshman year in 1996, to be coached by the famous G.A. Moore. From that moment on, my life hasn't been the same. Everybody has their memories of Coach Moore...victories, his fight for prayer before games and what he stood for...but mine was how he taught me that no matter what you do in life, 'Sucker, you've got to give it 110%,' and I have been living by that ever since. He taught me to always put God first, and everything else will fall into place. Because of Coach Moore's way of doing things, even the way he ran his coaching staff, it has impacted me more than words can describe...I love you, Coach Moore, and here's to you and what you stand for...thank you."

Another former player, Daric Gray, wrote to Coach Moore about the challenges and rewards he was experiencing at the United States Air Force Academy. "If there's anything

I remembered from high school ball, it is that suffering produces perseverance, perseverance produces character, and character produces hope (Romans 5:3). I wasn't very good when I started out at CHS (Celina High School), but I stuck with it and ended up coming through...Coach Moore, I just want you to know that I still remember every word you said to me and my teammates. Your teachings meant so much to me that I already have written one paper titled 'Being Orange' (Celina's colors) and another titled 'The Greatest Days of My Life' about my time as a Bobcat. I still have and will always have orange blood running through my veins."

Few Celina players had as much success on the field as Adam Herrin. He was the starting quarterback from 1998 through 2000 and led the team to three straight state championships. He earned a football scholarship to Rice University, where he beefed up and starred as a linebacker. Herrin wrote to Moore in 2012 when his wife was pregnant with their first son. "Do you think there's any chance you could come out of retirement in about fourteen years?" he wrote. "I wanted to let you know that so much of the winning attitude and pride that I now have as a man can be attributed to the things that you and your assistant coaches instilled in me in high school. So many of us that were part of those championship teams have maintained successful careers and have been blessed in ways that would not be possible had we not been part of something so great at Celina. I mean that from the bottom of my heart. For this, I will never be able to thank you enough."

In His Own Words...Childhood

Farming

Growing up, we worked ten hours a day. We'd start at seven in the morning, take an hour off for lunch from noon to one, and then work till six at night. We'd do that year 'round. We pulled cotton. We called it pulling bolls. We had to pull so much every day when I was a little bitty sucker. My mother was right there with us. She pulled cotton too. If we did real good and got two hundred pounds of cotton, our parents would let us go swimming in the tank. We worked real hard so we could go swimming.

We were poor, but we weren't poorer than anybody else, I guess. My mother and dad were not able to give me things that a lot of the kids nowadays have, but we were still blessed. We never had any money, but we had more fun than people that did have money. We worked together, played together, prayed together, and went to church together.

Horses on the Farm

When I was growing up, I rode horses all the time. One day, Daddy came home with a little spotted half-Shetland horse that hadn't been broke. I said, "Let me ride him." I was about six, I guess. He said, "No, he's going to throw you." I said, "No, he's not. I can ride anything." I kept arguing with him. Finally, Daddy turned around and slapped that horse on the butt and told me to go ahead. I rode him just a little ways, not very far. That sucker started bucking and threw me, and I landed head first in the sewer line. Of course, I got that junk all over me. My mother came out of the house, and she was screaming and hollering. She was running wide open down there. They dug me out of that thing. Mama carried me back to the house and pampered me. Daddy went back to the barn. Boy, she was mad as the dickens at him.

Growing Up in Mustang

I was born in Mustang, a little community between Pilot Point and Celina. The whole community helped raise me. We got a lot of whippings, and it wasn't just our family. The neighbors would whip you if you were acting wrong at their house. We had a community center, a little brick building that had been a school. Every Friday night, the whole community went down there and played 42. There were several tables. The kids learned to play 42 and got to play with some of them. They'd have Thanksgiving services down there and a community party at Christmas. People spent a lot of time at each other's houses, playing dominoes and things like that. You didn't go a lot of places, but you had fun in the community.

On Sunday afternoons, the moms would make ice cream, and we'd sit on the porch and eat it. There were acres and acres of open land where my friends and I would romp all day long. We'd saddle our horses in the morning and not come home until evening. There was always a creek or waterhole where we could go fishing. Life in the country was a grand place of adventure for me as a boy. I was privileged to know the great people of Mustang in my early years.

Kicked by a Cow

My dad ran a dairy when I was a little bitty kid. I started going to the barn when I was three and helping him milk the cows. Some people from the newspaper came out because they couldn't believe a kid who was three could milk cows. My dad taught me you walk up behind the cow, put your hand up on their hip, pat them, and let them know you're there. Then you can run your hand down by the bag, and you milk them. I'd always done that, but on this particular day – I guess I was trying to show off – I just ran up there and grabbed the tit. That cow kicked me and knocked me plumb back over on my head. About halfway knocked me out. My mother got pretty mad at Daddy over that. He had me doing things she didn't think I ought to be doing at that age.

My Dad, My Hero

Growing up, my dad was my idol. I thought he could do everything. He was kind of like my best friend. He was hard on me but, golly, he taught me so many things. We ran cattle and did everything together all the time. He quit school his senior year in high school. He got married when he was eighteen, and Mother was sixteen. Everyone else in his family had a college education, but he was the one they came to when they had problems because he had so much common sense.

I always thought if something happened to him, it would be the saddest day of my life. And it really was. My dad died in 1979. He was sixty-six, and he was still breaking horses. Matter of fact, he was breaking one for my son, Gary Don, when the horse went up and came back on him. The saddle horn ripped his ribs all apart. He broke his hip and his leg. They did surgery on him. He came home from the hospital and was getting around, walking and doing well, then he turned as yellow as could be. We took him back to the hospital. They didn't know what he had, but they said there was no cure. I got a feeling it was probably some bad blood. Back then, they didn't know what AIDS was.

Our theory was, he wouldn't have died if they hadn't given him that blood. The doctor wouldn't even sign the death certificate. He thought we were going to sue him for everything he had. We had to get the death certificate signed or my mother couldn't get insurance benefits. I looked him up and went to his house in Lewisville. I told him, "You are not going to get sued. Period. Don't worry about it." He signed the death certificate, but he was still scared, I think. My dad, boy, he could not stand people who sued other people. He just thought it was wrong and against biblical standards. Mother said the same thing. She said, "I'll live in poverty before I'll sue anybody." She did basically. She never did have anything.

My First Car

I got my first car when I was in the eighth grade. It was a Model A roadster. Daddy gave $135 for it. I had a paper route, and I made enough money to pay him back. I wrecked that thing when I was a freshman. It was the night before the first football game I ever played in high school. Troy Tomlin, Tucky Dunn, and I were going to Denton to see some girls and to watch some boys we knew play a junior high game. We were going down this road, old Highway 10. That Model A didn't go real fast, about thirty-five or forty miles per hour. It was a convertible, and we were playing a game where we threw old cleats we'd taken off our shoes into the air, then we'd drive under and catch them. It was stupid.

We went off the road a little bit, trying to catch those cleats, and ran square into a culvert. It was a wonder it didn't kill us. That thing spun in the air, came down, landed, and rolled backward. It tore it all to pieces. Tuck cut his chin all the way through. Troy had a busted head. It didn't hurt me. Anyway, we had to call my dad. Gosh dang, he was mad. He sold that car for whatever they'd give him for it. And I didn't have no car.

No Beer for Me

There was a lot of alcohol when I was growing up, but the group I ran with didn't drink. I was very, very fortunate in that I hated the taste of beer. I can only remember one time in my life it ever tasted good, and that's when I was working on a quarter horse ranch. We'd been out working some cows, and we were rolling wet in sweat. Joe Bob White, the guy that owned the ranch, drove down there, and he said, "You all look like you need something to drink. The only thing I've got is a beer." I drank that thing, and it was cold and wet. I said, "Lord a mercy, I never had one that tasted good, but that sucker tastes great."

Every other time, I didn't like it at all. I don't know if you know what Harry Truman said about beer: "As far as I'm concerned, you can pour it back in the horse." I told people that's kind of the way I felt about beer. My mother is

Moore standing beside friend's pickup at age thirteen, 1951

probably the reason I don't drink. She preached against drinking from the time I was big enough to walk. I've got some relatives that were alcoholics.

Chapter 8
Friday Nights in Texas

All across Texas, in towns big and small, Friday night football dominates.

The hard-hitting, fast-moving sport provides part of the appeal, but the allure extends far beyond tackles and touchdowns. The game played under the bright lights serves as a coming-of-age stage for a generation of eager teenagers. Boys, barely old enough to shave, carry the weighty expectations of their coaches, teammates, and community. They strap on helmets and shoulder pads and go to battle. Marching bands, high-kicking drill teams, and bouncy cheerleaders create a pulsating backdrop for the violence and beauty on the field.

More than 100,000 players take to the gridiron each fall in Texas – far more than in any other state. Not surprisingly, Texas produces more Division I college football players than any other state. High school football is played, with varying degrees of passion, throughout the United States. In some states, other youth sports – basketball, baseball, or soccer – outshine football. In Texas, football towers over all other high school sports. Kids who excel in football become icons – their names remembered for a generation or more.

Why are so many Texas teens – including gangly and untalented ones – drawn to play football? The answer is simple. Football offers tests and rewards that no other sport can match. In football, a kid finds out if he's tough enough to survive a two-hour practice in one hundred degree heat, clad in full pads. He finds out if he can whip a bigger opponent on the other side of the ball. He finds out what happens when he fails miserably, gets chewed out by his coach, and is dismissed by teammates. Will he slink away and quit the team? Or will he get up off the ground, stand tall, and hit somebody again?

Football teaches lifelong lessons: Mental toughness can trump talent. Failure can lead to success. Team victory is sweeter than individual glory. For generations, writers have been drawn to Texas to chronicle the pageantry and pathos of its unique brand of high school football.

"Football may be the American game, played by all ages and on all levels of competency, but nowhere does it excite passion, instill pride, and generate the intensity it does in Texas on the high school level," wrote Joe Nick Patoski (Patoski, Joe Nick. 2011). Patoski continued, "Like cattle, horses, and the weather, high school football is that rare subject that transcends language, economic status, ethnicity, faith, and geographic differences to bring folks together. It is a game, but it is also a participatory ritual celebrating team, school, and community." (Patoski, Joe Nick. 2011).

Texas high school football has a long, rich history. The first game was played December 24, 1892, in South Texas between Galveston's Ball High School and a local team called the Galveston Rugbys. The oddly named Rugbys, believed to be comprised of college-aged players, shut out the high schoolers, 14-0. The game "excited a degree of attention" and drew a "large concourse of people," according to a story in the *Galveston Daily News*. Football hadn't gained the sophistication it has today. The newspaper writer called the first game "mainly an exhibition of brute force."

Two years later, Ball High School, the Rugbys, and the Galveston YMCA formed the Galveston Football Association. The teams played each other several times, but also formed one team to play exhibition games in Texas cities such as Dallas, San Antonio, and Austin, according to the *Galveston Daily News*. "The exhibition games, which will be given from time to time, will afford sport to the public and keep aroused the spirit of interest among Galveston people," the paper stated, "With the number of players – about fifty – who will join, a most scientific and interesting development of football is to be expected."

High school football gradually took root in the Lone Star State. In 1901, Galveston Ball played Houston's Sam Houston High School. Sam Houston won, 23-6, in a game marred by several fights. Police eventually restored order. "Blows flew thick and fast," according to the *Houston Chronicle*, "For five minutes pandemonium reigned, until the two police officers on the scene were able to force their way through the struggling mass of humanity to the center of strife. The men were dragged from each other by main force."

Over the next decade, Texas high school football games became more orderly, and the number of teams mushroomed. Colleges such as the University of Texas, Texas A&M, Baylor, and Texas Christian had begun fielding football teams, fanning interest at the high school level. The first Texas high school championship was held December 13, 1913, between Houston Sam Houston and Comanche High School. "Houston, the pre-game favorite, jumped out to a 6-0 lead in the first quarter and added a pair of touchdowns in the final quarter to take a 20-0 victory over Comanche," wrote the *Houston Chronicle*. "Comanche almost scored in the second and third quarter but the Sam Houston defense stiffened...Comanche's loss was due to poor tackling and the powerful running of Sam Houston's [Marion] Settegast. [Frank] Litterest's darting runs also were difficult to stop."

As the game developed, several high school coaches began to make their mark. The first to achieve widespread renown was Paul Tyson of Waco in Central Texas. His coaching career spanned four decades, starting in 1912. During that time, he compiled a remarkable record of 229-

65-22 and won four state championships. He remained the state's winningest high school football coach for decades.

Tyson's teams dominated opponents. For instance, his 1921 Tigers team went undefeated and didn't allow a single point all year, while compiling 526 points. Only one team advanced the ball past midfield. In 1927, his team again went undefeated and beat Houston's Jeff Davis High School 124-0 in a playoff game – the largest postseason margin ever. "They would have beaten a good college team today," the losing coach said.

Legendary Knute Rockne, who coached Notre Dame to three national championships, once wrote that Tyson was "one of the finest coaches I ever met, college or high school." Yet, Tyson had no desire to leave Waco High and try his hand in college. No wonder. His team was so popular that it often drew more spectators than nearby Baylor University. What was his secret? He had a brilliant offensive mind. In an era of simple offensive plays, Tyson devised intricate plays that baffled opponents.

Tyson had as many as one hundred players on his teams – numbers that awed opponents. Players loved his soft-spoken approach. He motivated by sound instruction, not by yelling. It was an approach that would work for G.A. Moore decades later. Tyson "knew how to handle boys," a former player, Howard Dudgeon said. (Smith, Dave, ed. 1999). He went on to state, "He believed in discipline. If you started cussing, you didn't play the next game. If you made an error, he'd call you over...'Boy,' he'd say, 'this is what you did wrong. I know you can do better.'" (Smith, Dave, ed. 1999). Tyson's teams amassed mind-boggling statistics just as Moore's would. Eight times from 1921 to 1927, the Tigers scored one hundred or more points in a game. Twenty other times during that period, they scored seventy or more points. Waco won state championships in 1922, 1925, 1926, and 1927. The Tigers dominated the

1920s as no team has dominated a decade since. The 1927 team scored a record 784 points – a figure that wouldn't be surpassed for years.

Another coach built a formidable reputation in the early days of Texas football. Blair Cherry coached in Ranger, Fort Worth, and Amarillo from 1924 to 1936, compiling a record of 112-29-4. More significantly, he won three consecutive state championships from 1934 to 1936 while in Amarillo. During that span, his team lost only one game.

Like G.A. Moore many years later, Cherry had the highest standards for his players. He employed a swarming defense and explosive double-wing offense.

A reporter for the *Amarillo Daily News* observed practice and made this observation: "As the squad gradually absorbs Cherry's instructions on new plays and formations, they are continually brought to task for violation of some fundamental principle. And while they are gradually being built into a smooth-running machine, they are never permitted to lose sight of the little things."

In 1934, Amarillo won its first of three straight state championships, crushing favorite Corpus Christi, 48-0. Amarillo amassed 499 yards of offense, compared with only sixty-three for Corpus Christi. "It was one of those days where everything went right for us," former quarterback Johnnie Stidger told the *Amarillo Globe-News*. The next year, Amarillo won its second title with a narrow 13-7 win over Greenville. In 1936, Cherry's team completed a three-peat, downing Kerrville, 19-6. The coach's legendary preparation paid off. He noticed in scouting Kerrville that its punter took three steps, instead of the customary two, before kicking the ball. Amarillo players, armed with this information, managed to block two punts in the championship game, recovering both for touchdowns and providing the margin of victory. "It seemed like if we were going to play somebody, our knowledge of the team...was very good," an Amarillo player, Bill Thompson, said (Bynum, Mike, ed. 2003).

Cherry might have won many more titles if he had stayed in Amarillo. Instead, after the third championship, he became an assistant coach at the University of Texas in 1937. He spent a decade in that position before being named head coach at UT in 1947. He never matched his success at Amarillo, but he compiled a respectable 32-10-1 record before retiring after the 1950 season. His Longhorns won the Sugar Bowl in 1948, the Orange Bowl in 1949, and the Southwest Conference title in 1950.

Another Texas high school coach achieved legendary status during the 1930s. H.N. "Rusty" Russell led the Masonic Home, a school for orphans in Fort Worth, from 1927 to 1942, and he captured the public's imagination in a way few coaches have. The "Mighty Mites," as they were called, were mostly undersized, marginally talented players who didn't have the benefit of a supportive family. But Russell, in his role as father figure and coach, molded the unlikely players into a powerful team, routinely beating much larger schools with better athletes. Russell compiled a record of 132-27-9 at the Masonic Home. It included four undefeated regular seasons, six district championships, and an appearance in the state championship in 1932. The game ended in a scoreless tie, but the Mighty Mites lost on penetrations. In that game, they had only thirteen players on their roster.

One player, Dewitt "Tex" Coulter, said that Russell was "our guide and mentor. He was a great tactician." The coach was seen as an offensive genius, whose multiple formations confused opponents. Russell once told the *Houston Post*, "Shoot, I didn't go out there and wave a magic wand. We only had a few plays, but we ran them from a lot of different formations. We put a lot of men in motion, but I always figured if a wingback or end wasn't going to get the ball, he ought to be doing something to confuse a few people." (Smith, Dave, ed. 1999).

His 1941 team may have been his best. It went 9-0, scoring 244 points while allowing only thirty-two. It was featured in the popular *Colliers* magazine. But on the eve of the playoffs and a potential state championship, Russell discovered that one of his players was actually a year too old to be eligible. The Masonic Home was eliminated from postseason play. "When it came out and he told us, Coach cried a little bit," one player said (Bynum, Mike, ed. 2003). "I had never seen him shed a tear." Amazingly, two of the 1941 Mighty Mites, Coulter and Hardy Brown, went on to play in the NFL.

Russell coached the Masonic Home for only one more year. In 1942, the Mighty Mites finished 6-3 and missed the playoffs. He then coached at the much larger Highland Park High School near Dallas until 1944 before becoming an assistant coach at nearby Southern Methodist University. He took over as head coach from 1950 to 1952. During that stretch, his Mustangs upset Ohio State and Notre Dame.

His biggest impact, however, came as coach of the Mighty Mites. The Masonic Home has since closed, and Russell is remembered as the most inspirational leader in its long history.

In the 1950s another coach, Chuck Moser, dominated Texas High School football. He led Abilene High School from 1953 to 1959, compiling a record of 78-7-2 and winning three straight state championships. His teams also won forty-nine consecutive games – a record that remained until G.A. Moore's Celina Bobcats won their fiftieth in a row in 2001. Celina eventually extended the record to sixty-eight consecutive wins. Like Moore, Mosier is idolized by former players and fans.

"He was guide and guardian to all he coached, and his wisdom was so respected by players and their parents that no decree was too demanding, no invasion of privacy deemed offensive. Everyone knew his decisions were for the best of player and team, anyway. And everyone knew, in those days, that Coach Moser knew best...Moser didn't mind ordering one of his players to break up with a girlfriend. After all, if she was a bad girl, or if she distracted the player from his priorities of schoolwork and football, someone had to step in. At Abilene High School in the 1950s, Moser always had his eyes or his spies on his players." (Smith, Dave, ed. 1999).

Moser enforced a curfew on his players and demanded that they keep their hair cut short – just as Moore would do years later. Both coaches prepared detailed scouting reports on opponents and tested players on their assignments before games. "Chuck Moser was a great stickler for details," one of his assistant coaches said. "Moser was ahead of his time in so many ways. We ran a year-round program, and not many were doing that in those days," said a former player, "We knew every move the opponent had. He felt the more you knew, the better you'd be." (Smith, Dave, ed. 1999).

Abilene's forty-nine game winning streak came to an end on December 14, 1957, when it tied Highland Park, 20-20, in a semifinal game. Highland Park won on penetrations. Abilene might have kept the streak going if Moser hadn't held out two starters because they were each failing a class. Long before the state of Texas instituted a "no pass, no play" law, Moser had his own version. "The next morning, it was standing-room only at Moser's Sunday school class at St. Paul United Methodist Church as he spoke on the topic of lessons learned from losing a game...," wrote Al Pickett, sports editor of the *Abilene Reporter-News*.

Moser left the sidelines after the 1959 season. The school's football team never experienced the same success. Those who played during Moser's short but brilliant stint as head coach became known as "Chuck's Boys." Players and coach shared a mutual love.

Some coaches inspire admiration from players. Some inspire fear. Joe Golding, who coached Wichita Falls from 1947 to 1961, falls into the latter group. He had extraordinary success, achieving a record of 152-26-2 during that span. His teams appeared in six state championship games and won four – in 1949, 1950, 1958, and 1961. But few players loved Golding. "He was a tyrant," a former player, Jay Lavender, said. "He would get after your butt and make you do things you didn't want to do on your own." (Bynum, Mike, ed. 2003). Another player, Ed Beach, agreed. "In many ways, he was an impossible man to get along with. He was a harsh disciplinarian," he said. (Bynum, Mike, ed. 2003).

Moore at Celina football banquet surrounded by state championship trophy and awards for other playoff wins, 2000. Photo courtesy of Fred Helms

Golding's old-school methods would seem brutal today. Like some other coaches of his era, he didn't allow water breaks during marathon practices in one hundred degree heat. "The games were a relief," Beach said, "I never came out of a game as battered as I did in practice sessions. They couldn't do to us in a game what Joe Golding could do to us in four hours. I guess that's why his teams never got tired in the fourth quarter. He put you in such adversarial situations that anything we ran into in a game would be easier than what we had faced before."

Another player, Billy Bookout, said, "I don't know how we kept from dying." (Bynum, Mike, ed. 2003).

Golding, however, had plenty of football smarts in addition to his iron-fisted discipline. He was an offensive mastermind who could outsmart opposing coaches. "Joe was a great, great coach," a longtime assistant, Hunter Kirkpatrick, said, "We never went into a ballgame that our team didn't know what we were doing and what the other team was going to do. I don't care what kind of defense they played against us, we were going to operate some offense to beat it. His football system was as good as anybody's at the time." (Bynum, Mike, ed. 2003).

His first championship team in 1949 didn't lose a game all season. The next season, Wichita Falls lost four of its first five games but rebounded, made the playoffs, and ran the table to win a second straight title. Golding then had a championship drought until winning his two final state titles in 1958 and 1961.

Maybe Golding should be remembered for his results, not his harsh methods. Some of his former players, however, find it hard to forget the brutal practices that set Golding apart. "A lot of players would have quit," Beach said, "But they were too afraid of Golding to do it. They'd rather stay out there and suffer than face him."

Just as Golding was finishing his run of state championships, another coach was racking up titles – and he was doing it in a kinder, gentler way. Gordon Wood won his first championships in 1955 and 1956 in Stamford in north central Texas, then he moved 120 miles south and won an astounding seven titles in Brownwood from 1960 to 1981. Before Coach Moore, Wood was the winningest Texas High School football coach.

Wood's nine championships remain a state record. Moore came close to reaching him with eight. Moore, however, surpassed Wood's win total of 396 in 2002. Moore, who retired in 2011, finished his career with 429 victories. Unlike Golding, a taskmaster, Wood was a patient instructor.

He disagreed with the notoriously intense practices of famed college coach Paul "Bear" Bryant. In 1954, Bryant was hired to rebuild the football program at Texas A&M University. Before the season began, he held a ten day camp four hours from the university. Even though the temperature topped one hundred degrees, Bryant denied his players water and kept them on the field from before dawn to dark. More than half the team quit before the agonizing camp ended. Bryant, who later won six national championships at the University of Alabama, believed that the excruciating workouts toughed his A&M squad. To Wood, however, Bryant's approach had more negative effects than positive.

"[T]he cruel coaching methods he sanctioned at Junction in 1954 ruined more coaches and did more damage to Texas football than any coach before or since," Wood wrote in his 2001 autobiography, *Coach of the Century*. "Bryant was much too rough on players, but because he was so successful, many young coaches chose to emulate his coaching style…" (Carver, John and Gordon Wood. 2001).

Wood started his coaching career in Rule in central Texas in 1940 and stayed for two years. After a stint in the Navy in World War II, Wood coached in Roscoe, Seminole, and Winters before landing in Stamford in 1951. There in the Texas Panhandle, Wood made his mark. He won back-to-back state championships in 1955 and 1956 and compiled an 80-6 record in seven seasons.

After a two-year stint in Victoria, Wood took over in Brownwood in central Texas. He became a legend there, just as Moore became a legend in Celina. From 1960 until he retired in 1985, Wood won seven state championships and 257 games in Brownwood. He never had a losing season. Like Moore, Wood was known for squeezing every ounce of talent out of his players, most of whom never played a down after high school. He also hated mistakes. "He could motivate kids to do things they didn't think they could do," Wood's longtime assistant, Morris Southall, said. "He had the players ready for every situation that might arise." (Bynum, Mike, ed. 2003).

Wood and Moore each grew up on a farm and, despite their success, had an "aw-shucks" humility that was genuine and endearing. Both preached perfection. "It's not the big things that beat you," Wood told the *Dallas Morning News*. "It's a million little things." Like Moore, he created an expectation for winning among players and fans. "We sell our players on the idea they can win the state championship every year," Wood said.

Moore met Wood at a coaching clinic, and the two became close friends. When Moore neared his victories mark, Wood cheered him on. In his later years, in failing health, Wood attended some of Moore's playoffs games to encourage him to break the record. Moore may have surpassed Wood in victories, but he places himself behind Wood as a coach. Wood died in 2003, a year after Moore set the victories record. Wood and Moore are the only two Texas High School coaches to win state championships in four different decades.

"I'm not even in his league," Moore told the Associated Press as he neared Wood's record. "It doesn't matter if somebody wins five hundred games, we're not going to reach his level. It's kind of like looking back at Tom Landry or Vince Lombardi. That's how he affected high school football."

Some Texas High School coaches didn't win nearly as many games as Wood and Moore, but they still had lasting impacts. For instance, Emory Bellard posted a record of 177-59-9 and won three state championships during twenty-one years as a high school coach. His first stint lasted from 1952 to 1966. During that time, he won titles at Breckenridge in 1958 and 1959 and at San Angelo in 1966. He returned to high school coaching from 1988 to 1993, leading Spring Westfield High School near Houston.

Between the two high school stints, Bellard made a name for himself as a college coach. As an assistant at the University of Texas in 1968, Bellard created the triple option, or Wishbone offense, that Texas used to win the 1969 and 1970 national championships. Many other high-profile college programs, such as Oklahoma, picked up the offense and had great success too. Bellard became a successful head coach as well. He led Texas A&M from 1972 to 1978, achieving two ten-win seasons, and Mississippi State from 1979 to 1985, earning a spot in two bowl games.

Bum Phillips is best known as an NFL coach. He led the Houston Oilers from 1975 to 1980, twice taking them to the AFC championship game. He then coached the New Orleans Saints from 1981 to 1985. But before achieving national fame, Phillips served as a Texas high school coach for thirteen seasons. "I'm as proud to have been a high school coach in Texas as I am to have gone on to the NFL," he wrote. "It was at the high school level – at Nederland, Port Neches, Jacksonville, and Amarillo – where I learned how to be a professional coach." (Cashion, Ty. 1998).

Phillips became head coach at Nederland High School on the Texas gulf coast in 1951 at age twenty-seven. He compiled a record of 53-16-3 in six seasons, leading the team to quarterfinal appearances in 1953, 1954, and 1955 and the state title game in 1956. Phillips also coached at Jacksonville in 1958, at Amarillo from 1959 to 1961, and at Port Neches-Grove in 1963 and 1964.

Phillips always credited his high school coaching experience for the success he had at higher levels. "When I got to the college and professional level, I didn't really change anything," he wrote. "At the bottom line, I still tried to get every young man to do better than he thought he was capable of doing. To do that, you've got to understand him and truly know him, or you can't get him to perform at a notch higher than he thinks he can." (Cashion, Ty. 1998).

Until recently, Art Briles was known as one of college football's top coaches. However, his successful tenure at Baylor University ended abruptly when he was fired in May 2016 after a school-commissioned report outlined several sexual assaults committed by Baylor players. After taking over at Baylor in 2008, Briles resurrected the program, winning the Big 12 title twice and regularly being ranked in the Top 25. In 2011, his quarterback, Robert Griffin III, became the first Baylor athlete to win the coveted Heisman Trophy as college football's top player. Briles built explosive offenses offenses. In 2014, Baylor led Division I schools by amassing an average of 48.2 points and 581.5 yards per game.

But before Briles forged his reputation in college, he was considered one of the all-time great Texas high school football coaches. In sixteen years at three schools, he went 166-46-4 and won four state championships. All the titles came at Stephenville High School, where he coached from 1988 to 1999. He developed an offensive prowess that he would later bring to Baylor. In 1993 and 1994, he won back-to-back state championships while relying mainly on a running attack. His teams scored a total of 185 rushing touchdowns in those two seasons. Later in the decade, Briles switched to a passing offense and won consecutive titles in 1998 and 1999 while shattering offensive records. Six of his quarterbacks, including former NFL starter Kevin Kolb, were awarded scholarships to Division I colleges.

Before Briles became Stephenville's coach in 1988, the school hadn't been to the playoffs in more than three decades. During his tenure, the Yellow Jackets became a dynasty.

He instituted a rigorous offseason program, just as Moore did at Celina. Briles and Moore have become friends over the years. Briles says he admires Moore for remaining a high school coach and influencing young players to perform well on the field and act right off the field. "The record speaks for itself," Briles says. "A lot of coaches put a whistle around their neck, but for him to be No. 1 is an astonishing achievement. More importantly, he is a man of character and faith. To me, that's as impressive as his wins – the way he won those games and the players he developed through all those years. You have to have a plan, a method, a concept and stick with it. G.A. has done that. If players step on the field and expect to win, which his teams did, your probability of a positive outcome certainly increases. Somebody will break his record, possibly, some day. But nobody can ever change the influence he's had."

Some coach will break Moore's record – and it will be Phil Danaher of Calallen High School in South Texas. It won't be long either. Danaher has had a remarkable run at the school, starting in 1984 and continuing to the present. He has compiled 418 wins – only eleven shy of Moore's mark – and has lead the team to the playoffs for thirty-one consecutive years.

Danaher could surpass Moore's wins record during the 2016 season, but for all his success he's never won a state championship. Moore, by comparison, won eight. "I'd love to have his state championship record," says Danaher, who is a decade younger than Moore. "G.A. Moore did a great job. He's a good man and a great coach."

Danaher's Wildcats have come close to winning it all. They've been to one state championship game and ten semifinals – and lost each time. In five consecutive years in the mid-1990s, Calallen lost to the same team, La-Marque. Once, the game went to overtime. Another time, LaMarque won in the last minute. A third agonizing time, LaMarque won on the game's final play.

"Winning state is part luck," Danaher says. "Maybe we're better than we are lucky. Still, how many coaches can say they've been to five semifinals? It would be great to win a state championship. I'd love to cherish that moment. But if it doesn't happen, it doesn't happen. I can look in the mirror and say, 'I did everything I could to get there.' We might not have a state championship, but we have one of the most consistent programs ever."

Like Moore, Danaher sees his job description as much more than winning games. He and Moore have similar personalities and approaches to coaching. Both believe in building up kids, not tearing them down, and teaching them life lessons, not just how to make the perfect tackle.

"I guess I'm not as hard as most coaches because kids are kids. They're going to make mistakes," Danaher says. "I tell my coaches every year, 'We want the kids to achieve, but treat kids like you'd want your kid treated.' Football is such a team sport. That's what I really like about the game – the unity it teaches, how important it is for everybody to carry out their assignment. Sometimes a kid needs athletics more than athletics needs that kid. It might straighten him up. You never know what one of these kid's home life is like. We're there for the kids – not necessarily to make heroes out of all these guys."

He never cuts a player, no matter how little talent he might have. He recalls one special needs player he once had. "He couldn't remember the plays. He didn't know where to go. That's all right. I couldn't cut a kid like that. If he wants to come to practice and be part of the team, so be it."

Years ago, Danaher had six players off a single team earn college football scholarships. Yet the team never jelled and didn't advance far in the playoffs. The next year, no one received a scholarship – but the team went all the way to the state finals. "You can't win with great athletes," Danaher says. "Great athletes already know they're great and don't work to get better. Motivation is the biggest thing. You outwork the guy next to you. Who would you rather go to battle with – someone who's going to fight or someone who thinks he's going to win no matter what? I'm always harder on kids who have more talent because you've got to push them to be better. A kid who knows he's not real talented will work on his own to get better."

Danaher, like Moore, hates mistakes and is a stickler for order. "We're disciplined on the field and in the field house," he says. "Being disciplined on the field, like I tell coaches, doesn't mean yelling at kids. It means when you see a kid make a mistake, correct it then. Don't say, 'I'll catch it the next time he does it.' When you go into the locker room, we have a picture of how a locker should look. You put your shirt on this hook, your shorts on this hook, your game shoes in the right corner, your practice shoes in the left corner. It's all part of being disciplined."

Discipline leads to success on the field, Danaher believes. "At Calallen, it's not acceptable to lose." He wears a cap that says, "Where Winning is a Tradition." Danaher has coached many outstanding players, including his two sons, Cody and Wes. Cody, whose senior year was 1991, earned a scholarship to the University of Texas and started several games at safety. Wes, who was a senior in 1995, went to Southern Methodist University on scholarship, but a back injury cut short his career as a running back. In high school, however, he had extraordinary success, setting the state record for rushing yards in Calallen's classification with 8,855 yards. He earned induction into the Texas High School Hall of Fame in 2013.

When Phil Danaher coached Wes, he faced the challenge of giving him enough carries to set the state record – while still letting other runners have the ball. In practice, he made a point of not being too easy on his son. He realizes he may have gone overboard and times and been too demanding. "One time, we're in the playoffs, and Wes wasn't practicing well. He was messing up because he wasn't concentrating. I said, 'Get off the field! I don't care if you play another down for us.' My defensive coordinator said, 'Coach, we have a hundred or so players here. You can coach them all you want and tell them they're not going to play another down. But leave Wes to us. We'll coach him.' That Friday night, Wes rushes for six touchdowns and two hundred something yards. I said, 'OK, I see your point.'"

Danaher credits his assistant coaches and players for his wins, rather than taking the credit himself. "I'm not the smartest coach in the world by far, but I've always had a knack for being able to hire good people. I believe I could learn from anybody. When I'm talking to a coach, I want to know what he knows. What good is it for me to tell him what I know?"

The Calallen school board honored Danaher in 2009 by naming the stadium after him. He has no plans to retire. "I enjoy coaching. I love kids. I've got the greatest job in the world. I look forward to coming to work every day. When it's no fun anymore – that's when I'll get out."

In His Own Words...Ranching

Bucked Again

A while back, I was putting up a young horse, one I'd raised. He always bucked a little every time I got on him, but it wasn't any big deal. I got down to the gate and was going to check on some cows. I got off and opened the gate. When I started to get back on, I put my foot in the stirrup and, boy, he jerked straight back. I flew off and landed on my shoulder. Tore that thing all to pieces. Makes me so mad. A few years ago, that wouldn't have even hurt me.

They X-rayed it and did surgery. This sweet old gal – I've known her for some time – sat me down and said, "Don't be lifting any weights for six months. Don't be doing anything out there on that ranch. And don't be throwing no footballs." She said it was all pulled loose in there, and it's screwed back down. It's amazing what they can do. A few years ago, I guess you'd be a cripple if you did this.

Charging Bull

Jersey bulls are mean suckers. We'd raised this one, and I let him run with the heifers. One time, he didn't want me to go out in the big pasture. I got out a whip and was popping him. He shook his head and pawed the ground. I kept on and, boy, he came after me. I went down to the ground and rolled under the fence. He was butting me and rolling me. I don't know exactly how all that happened, except that bull was on top of me. I finally got into the golf cart, but he was still fighting, trying to get to me. My wife was on top of the gate, hollering. She got up in the golf cart and brought me to the house.

All the hide was gone off the side of my head and arms, and one of my legs was just raw all the way down. They had to do some skin grafts. That bull surprised me a little bit because he was a pet we'd raised and roped with. But he just turned on me. My oldest girl is a cowgirl. We have a big trailer, and she got that bull to chase her into the trailer. She went out the front and locked the door. She took him that afternoon to the auction in Muenster. She told that guy to sell him for whatever they could get. Bulls are like that. We've got sixteen right now, and two will fight you if you hem them up.

Raising Cattle

We've always had cattle. I love getting on a horse and going and working cattle. For years and years, my dad and I ran cattle together. I'm running seven pastures now, and there's about 2,800 acres all together – two hundred acres of that is all I own. It's part of the old home place, been here since 1912. My granddad and his brother used to own all this around in here. It's been split up and sold off. When they came in, they were farming with mules and horses, then they went to tractors.

Now, we have about three hundred mother cows and sixteen bulls. It's really too big an operation just for me. We lost two calves and doctored two just yesterday. Ain't no use worrying about it. Daddy always told me, "If you don't have them, you can't lose them." If you're going to run cattle, you're going to lose some. This is kind of like coaching. If you didn't love this stuff, it would be a terrible lifestyle.

Surprise Snake Bite

About 1980, I was up here in the barn one day. We were hauling hay, my wife and I, and we had these bales stacked up. I stepped between the bales, and I thought a piece of wire stuck me in the leg. I felt it, but I didn't think anything about it. I went about my business, and that night my leg kind of swelled up. I laid here on the couch and put it up and put some ice on it. About three days later, I was over here in the roping pen, and my old leg swelled up again and got blue. I got on a horse, and it locked up. My wife took me to the doctor. They stretched it out and as soon as they looked at it, they said, "You've been snake bit."

I didn't even know that. The fang marks were on the back side, and I'd never looked at them. Evidently, there were some copperheads in the hay. I told this guy, "I went three days before it got so bad I couldn't move it, and I kept thinking I could take care of it." He said, "You had some boots on, and that snake hit you right on top of the boots. I would guess he struck several times and shot venom out before he got to your leg. You didn't get a very big dose of venom. He very easily could have killed you." Of course, if I had known what it was, I would have gone to the doctor. I had no idea. When it locked up, I thought I was having a stroke.

Castrating Bulls

We castrate bulls so they don't run around bothering the cows all the time. That way, they can concentrate on gaining weight. We castrate them at about two or three months. Buyers will give a little more for steers than bulls. Their meat is just a little better to eat. Bulls have a tendency to muscle up. We use rubber bands now to castrate them. We used to use a knife. You put that rubber band around the top of their balls, and the blood shuts off, and the bag dries up. It falls off after about two or three weeks. It's probably not very much fun, but it's not as bad as cutting them, I don't think.

Chapter 9
Beyond Football

G. A. Moore received many honors throughout his legendary coaching career, but the biggest came six months after he retired. In spring 2012, Moore was inducted into the Texas Sports Hall of Fame in Waco, near the campus of Baylor University.

Moore joined an induction class that included Mack Brown, then head football coach at the University of Texas, and Lovie Smith, then coach of the NFL's Chicago Bears. Both had reached the pinnacle of their professions: Brown had won a national championship at Texas, and Smith had coached the Bears to the Super Bowl. In his acceptance speech, Moore said he felt humbled to be in such esteemed company. The hall includes more than three hundred other inductees, such as former NFL stars Roger Staubach, Troy Aikman, and Emmitt Smith. "If you talk about feeling unworthy, that's the way I feel," Moore said to the large crowd. "I kind of feel like a fish out of water."

Many of his former players, coaching colleagues, and friends would disagree. To them, Moore is as deserving as anyone enshrined in the Texas Sports Hall of Fame. Few, if any, inductees excelled for as long as Moore did or influenced as many lives. D.W. Rutledge, executive director of the Texas High School Coaches Association, believes Moore earned a spot among the greatest players and coaches in Texas history. "He's a hero to a bunch of us coaches," says Rutledge, who won four Texas high school football championships as a coach. "The thing that I admired about G.A. was that he was in coaching for the right reasons. He wanted to develop better men first and better athletes second."

Moore working cattle on his ranch, 1981

Moore is normally reserved in public, not given to rah-rah speeches or stirring recollections of his coaching highlights. On the night of his induction, Moore found the perfect mix of humility and humor in a speech that captivated attendees. He talked about running his two hundred acre ranch, smack dab between Celina and Pilot Point, the towns where he achieved most of his coaching victories. It's land that his grandfather bought more than a century ago and where Moore grew up picking cotton. He talked about growing up with strict parents. "They'd be in jail now because they beat the dog out of me all the time." He talked about going to church regularly as a child – whether he wanted to or not. "I had a bad drug problem. I got drug to church every Sunday morning, and I got drug to church every Sunday night, and I got drug to church every Wednesday night. Thank goodness, the Lord knew that Mama and Daddy needed a lot of help."

He closed his speech by thanking his players, assistant coaches, and family. "I wish I could express to everybody who's been associated with me how much I really love them. Money can't buy what I've got, and it's because of these people here tonight. There's not anybody who will ever be up here that will deserve it less than me. But I'll tell you this: There will never be anybody inducted into this thing that will appreciate it and love the privilege as much as I have. Thank you very much."

Moore's induction gave football fans throughout Texas a chance to savor his legacy. In Celina and Pilot Point, Moore is idolized and discussed frequently. Moore may be in his seventies, but he retired too soon in the eyes of some. Could he come out of retirement and patrol the sidelines again? He's tempted occasionally, but a return is unlikely given his health problems. In 2013, Moore had three back surgeries to repair damage caused by years of nonstop activity – rodeoing, playing football with abandon, scurrying around the field instructing players, and galloping on his horse across the ranch. Moore used crutches for months during intensive rehabilitation until one day he said, "Enough." He tossed the crutches in his closet and closed the door. Pain be damned, he resolved to stand up straight and go about his business – whether it be riding a tractor or driving down bumpy country roads to the feed store.

G.A. Moore isn't the sedentary type. He likes to get out, in large part, to see his buddies. He has buddies at the cattle auction, where he frequently buys and sells bulls and heifers. They view him more as a rancher than a former football coach. "He's a better rancher as far as I'm concerned," says Robert Smithers, who works at a cattle auction near Moore's ranch. "Some of us don't even care that he coached." Moore has buddies throughout Celina and Pilot Point – men of all ages who greet him with a firm handshake or a hug, eager to share memories or talk about the current high school team.

Moore loves his family, first and foremost. One of his daughters and her husband live in a house next door on the ranch. His other two daughters and son live only minutes away. Most Sundays, they all gather for dinner in

Moore with wife, Lois Ann, and children.
Left to right: Carol, Tona, Gary Don, and Pam

Moore's modest home. "We have a family reunion every week," he says. The grandchildren call him "Big Dad." To his kids and grandkids, Moore was a great football coach – the best ever, of course, but their deep-seated love for him has nothing to do with his accomplishments on the field. Moore managed to win hundreds of football games and leave an everlasting mark on his profession without sacrificing his family life.

His wife of fifty-five years, Lois Ann, says she loves him more than ever. "He is a kind, loving, and very compassionate gentleman. I have lived the life of a teenager all these years – years filled with high school events and high school friends. He is always in charge of any situation. He knows the best way to handle it, and he takes care of it. My heart explodes with joy to be in his presence. He is my life."

His children also adore him. Gary Don, as the only son, shares a special bond with his father. He learned football from him, from the time he could walk. With Gary Don quarterbacking, the two won a state championship together at Celina in 1995. Today Gary Don is an assistant coach at a nearby school and often calls his dad for advice. He tries to follow the example his dad set in treating players. "Most coaches will baby stud players and embarrass the guy who doesn't even know if he wants to be out there," Gary Don says. "My dad was the opposite. He rode the heck out of studs. The guys who didn't really know if they wanted to be out there – he'd put his arm around them, trying to help them. He knew it was going to make a better life for them just being part of the team."

Gary Don, who is in his late thirties, hopes to be a head coach himself one day. He believes he had the best mentor imaginable in his father. "I'm so blessed to know what I know because of him. I got the bonus of knowing all the Xs and Os it took him forever to learn. But being able to build relationships with kids is still the most important thing."

If G.A. Moore's only goal had been to win games, he could have spent his entire career in either Celina or Pilot Point, foregoing the back and forth and building a single dynasty. In retirement, he's sometimes asked how many games he could have won if he'd stayed in one place. Perhaps five hundred or more, instead of 429?

But if Moore had concentrated only on victories, he wouldn't be as revered as he is today. Each time he went back to a struggling Pilot Point or Celina program, he not only reinvigorated the team, he impacted young men and the entire community. He taught a new group about respecting others, believing in themselves, and trusting God. Those 429 wins and eight state championships are remarkable accomplishments. Molding boys into men of character – that was G. A. Moore's real legacy as a coach.

***

These days, Moore is still coaching a team, of sorts. He's pastor of Mustang Baptist Church, a white-frame country church a half-mile from his ranch. He grew up in the church and has fond memories of accepting Christ there during a revival as an eight-year-old. In recent years, the church's membership steadily dwindled as people moved away or died. Only four members remained in spring 2015, and they considered donating the building to another church. That's when one of them, Dale Redfearn, reached out to Moore.

He knew that Moore had taught Sunday School and done some guest preaching over the years. Plus, he'd presided at funerals and led Fellowship of Christian Athletes meetings. Redfearn, who also attended Mustang Baptist Church as a child, thought Moore would be the perfect person to save the church. Moore was driving by the church in his pickup one day when Redfearn flagged him down. He pitched his idea. "I said, 'I've got to have some help.' I knew if anybody could get people to come here, it would be him. There was no doubt in my mind he could do it." Moore expressed some interest but didn't make any commitment. He had plenty to do with running the ranch, but he promised that he and Lois Ann would pray about it. They did, and both felt God wanted him to take over the church. Lois Ann would support him fully, just as she supported him in coaching all those years.

A year after Moore became pastor, Mustang Baptist Church is undergoing a resurgence. Sunday attendance, once in the single digits, now regularly approaches one hundred. Moore has started Wednesday night prayer meetings and held several gospel singing sessions on Saturday night. Members bring desserts and invite nearby residents. Volunteers have spruced up the aging church building, giving it new windows, siding, flooring, and roofing. The sign out front bears his name – beside pastor, it says "Coach G.A. Moore." The church, under Moore's leadership, now exudes life instead of decline. "There's no doubt in my mind the church was saved by him," says Redfearn. "The good Lord probably had a little hand in it too."

Moore never envisioned being a pastor at this stage of his life, but it seems fitting. After all, he quit coaching briefly in 1971 with the idea of attending seminary and pursuing the ministry. God, however, redirected his path back into coaching after only a year away. Now he believes God has lead him back to the ministry – lo, these many years later.

Moore with his wife, children, and extended family at the church he pastors, 2015. Photo courtesy of Ed Housewright

"I feel like I'm doing what I'm supposed to do," he says. "I couldn't be happier. We've got some people who are really excited about our church. Some of them I never even dreamed would show up. I look forward to Sundays just like I used to look forward to Friday nights."

Some of the regular attendees are his own kids and grandkids. Moore didn't have to ask them to leave their own churches – they did so voluntarily. "That's just how our family is," Gary Don says. "I don't think we ever gave it a second thought. That's what we all wanted to do immediately. It's been amazing for our family, all going to the same church."

Moore starts working on his sermon early in the week, making notes that he carries with him on Sunday. Lois Ann serves as his advisor, helping him shape the message. He sprinkles his sermons with football metaphors and stories. He sees many parallels between athletics and spirituality. "You've got to have discipline to do what you ought to do," Moore says. "You try to get athletes to commit to be the best athlete they can be. It's the same way with being a Christian. If you're really going to be the kind of Christian you should be, you can't do the smoking and drinking and partying and carousing and cussing and all that kind of stuff," he adds.

Members say Moore's preaching is straightforward and motivational. "When I heard he was going to be the pastor, I thought, 'He was a good football coach. People listened to him. I'll bet he'd be a good pastor too,'" says Patti Dellenbaugh. "I like the small country atmosphere. It's simple. I just want somebody to read the Scripture and explain what it means in today's world. I'd gotten away from church recently. Now, I look forward to getting up on Sunday instead of sleeping in."

Moore has tapped many of his longtime friends to fill leadership positions in the church. Morris Morgan, the father of one of Moore's star players in the 1980s, teaches the adult Sunday school class. Junior Worthey, a standout player in the 1960s, is Sunday school superintendent. Worthey and his wife, Verna, were two of the first people to join the church after Moore became pastor. "It's been amazing," Verna says. "He's preaching the word of God, and I think it is touching people's hearts. We're trying to reach out to the community and show them love. People respond to that." Junior says, "G.A. wants to be successful in anything he does. He's not going to go into anything halfway. He's there to make this church go if it's God's will."

On a recent Sunday, Moore's sermon was titled simply "Eternal Life." In the bulletin, Moore printed the "ABC's of Salvation: A. Admit that you are a sinner; B. Believe that Jesus died for your sins and is waiting to save you; C. Confess to the Lord that you are a sinner and ask Him to come and live in your heart and be your Savior." The service included the classic hymns "The Old Rugged Cross" and "Just As I Am."

Moore recently performed his first wedding in the church. Michael and Judi Colwick, who live down the road, asked Moore to do the service. They had just started attending Mustang Baptist Church and were struck by Moore's compassion and the strength of his preaching. They didn't know anything about his coaching background. "The more time I spent around G.A. and Lois Ann and the people of the church, the more I started falling in love with them," Michael says. Moore counseled with Michael and Judi before marrying them but wouldn't accept any money for performing the service. "As a matter of fact, they took up a collection from the church and gave us two hundred dollars as a wedding gift," Michael says. "That really touched my heart. It made me cry."

Members and observers see a bright future for the church. It's about forty-five minutes north of Dallas in a rapidly growing area. Hundreds of homes are being built nearby. "He's sitting right in the middle of an explosion," says Luther Slay, a retired Baptist preacher and longtime friend of Moore. "If he can build a good foundation right now with the group that he's got and then keep reaching out to the humongous number of families that are going to be moving in, there's no reason that church can't just go through the roof."

Slay met Moore more than fifty years ago. He was pastoring Calvary Baptist Church in Pilot Point when Moore was a young coach. Even then, Moore had his eye on the ministry. "This is something that he's been wanting to do for years and years and years. I can remember when he was much younger, he came to me in my office, and we talked a long time about it. This isn't something he did on the spur of the moment. It's something that's been building for all his life, really. I'm so proud of him. He's happy in what he's doing. He's really in it hook, line, and sinker," Slay says.

Moore is so committed to the church that he's scaling back his ranch, which has been a lifelong love. He's reduced his head of cattle from about three hundred to two hundred. The church has taken some of his focus off the ranch – and off thoughts of returning to coaching. Even now, Moore believes he could coach again. "I would *love* to coach," he says. But he thinks about his church duties and the obligation he has made to members and to the Lord. "The only way I would coach would be if I could still preach, and I don't think I could do both. That might be too much. Preaching is more important."

How long can Moore continue to pastor the church? He doesn't know. "I haven't even thought about it." Others have. "I can see him doing this for a long time – until he can't anymore physically," says daughter Tona Van-Hook-Drees. Brian Lynn, who is married to another of Moore's daughters, thinks G.A. will keep preaching "until he passes away. It's all or nothing with him. He doesn't vacation. He doesn't fish. He doesn't golf."

Lynn has a special relationship with Moore. He met the coach when he was a small, slow wide receiver and cornerback in the early 1980s at Pilot Point. With Moore's motivation, Lynn worked and worked and wound up making the all-district team. He also got up enough courage to ask Moore if he could take his daughter Carol to the junior prom. Lynn didn't consider asking Carol without first getting Moore's permission. Why? "Because he was G.A. Moore. I thought that's what a young man was supposed to do. It was just the respect I had for him." The coach allowed Brian to take Carol to the dance. "He said she had to be home by a certain time. I already knew that."

Two years later, Brian again approached Moore. This time, he asked if he could marry her. He never actually asked Carol. "I asked G.A., and he said absolutely. He told Lois Ann and Lois Ann told Carol."

Lynn spent twenty years as a firefighter. Now he's retired, and he and Carol live next door to G.A. and Lois Ann. Lynn is a leader in the church. He gives the announcements each Sunday morning during the service. Few people respect G.A. Moore as much as Brian Lynn. Both his parents are dead, and he views Moore as a friend, father, and spiritual leader. "He changed and directed my life in a way that I didn't think anybody could. I came from a pretty harsh background. We were poor, and I guess people looked down on us. There was always drama. My extended family was always in trouble with the law. I'd use the word 'outlaws.' I never went to church until my sophomore year. G.A. asked me if I'd go to a FCA (Fellowship of Christian Athletes) summer camp. He told me, 'I really, really think it would benefit you.' Lo and behold, it did."

Lynn is one of countless people G.A. Moore has influenced over the decades. He made his reputation in coaching, but winning ballgames alone doesn't earn a man the admiration Moore has achieved. He's always had a higher calling. Now, in the final quarter of his life, Moore's calling has extended to winning souls and comforting the flock.

Members of the church call him Coach Moore – not Pastor Moore or Reverend Moore or Brother Moore. He'll always be Coach Moore. G.A. Moore is a coach in the fullest, finest sense of the word.

Moore in pulpit at Mustang Baptist Church.
Photo courtesy of Ed Housewright

In His Own Words...
Friends, Family, and God

Count Your Friends

I've always been told if you've got four or five friends that
stick with you through everything, then you're a fortunate person. I've found that out by what I've done, going
back and forth between Celina and Pilot Point. I've got
more than five friends, but not a whole lot more than that.

The Greatest Coach's Wife

I don't know how many people have told me over the
years that Lois Ann is the perfect coach's wife. She did all
the little things that so many women married to a coach
don't realize you have to do. She knew every kid. She
knew their parents. The last several years, she thought
she knew as much about football as I did. If I went back to
coaching now, she'd be one hundred percent for it. That's
just the way she is. She loves football. I never had any
problems at home like a lot of coaches do

Lois Ann always made sure nobody bothered me when I
was looking at film in the back room. The reason she got
so good at feeding the cows and horses is because I'd be
in here working, and she'd have all the work done at the
barn. Lois Ann is the greatest thing that's ever happened
to me. I tell people, "Before you hire a coach, you'd better
talk to the wife." I learned that a long time ago.

Working Hard to Get a House

I never made a lot of money coaching football. The most I
ever made was $75,000. One time, a house became avail-
able for sale in Pilot Point. I loved that place, and we

wanted it, but we didn't have any money. So that summer, we had five jobs as a family. I coached, ran a ranch for a federal judge, ran another ranch for a lawyer, sold life insurance, and my wife and kids hired out as janitors where we went to church. A friend and I set a record for the most life insurance sales ever in a two-month period for Franklin Life Insurance Co.

Every day after I got off work selling insurance, I went home and checked the ranches. The reason we took those jobs was because we wanted something, and the only way we could get it was to work for it. We got that house. It was a beautiful house.

Pulling Pam's Tooth

When my oldest daughter was five or six, she had a loose tooth in front. I told her, "We need to pull that tooth." She said, "No, I don't want you to pull it. I'll get it out." She came home from school the next day, and she still hadn't done it. A day or two later, she still hadn't done it. I told her, "Pam, you'd better have it pulled tomorrow or I'm going to pull it with a pair of pliers." Well, she still didn't do it, so I pulled it out with some pliers. Oh, she cried. Her mother hugged on her and patted her. I had to go outside. Boy, it liked to kill me. I shouldn't have done that, and I did it to my own child. That's when I quit saying, "If you don't do this, this is what I'm going to do." I promised myself then I wouldn't ever paint myself into a corner again.

Accepting Jesus

All the kids I grew up with were good Christians and came from good families. We all went to church. Golly, we never missed. My mother and dad were big members of the Mustang Baptist Church. I could pick up a rock from the road in front of our house and nearly hit it. Every time there was a revival in the summertime, the preacher stayed at our house. There was always a service in the morning at ten and a service at night. I was always real glad to see those revivals because I got to get out of the cotton patch.

As a boy, I had a tendency to be a bit ornery. I remember the preacher and other adults pulling me aside and telling me I needed Christ. My mother also spoke to me quite a bit about Christ. I can be a bit hard-headed at times, so I just kept putting off my decision. The day before the revival ended – I was eight – my dad went to town to buy some things. He looked over at me and said, "Son, are you thinking about making a decision to accept Christ?" That's what I did – I decided on the worn-out seat of our pickup truck that I would make Christ my Lord. I'd been thinking about it for a while, but when my dad told me that's what I needed to do, that settled my mind and heart.

The next morning at church, I went down the aisle during the invitation to talk to the preacher. We talked, and he told me to kneel down at the front pew. I can say I never felt better about any other decision. My mother used to change the sheets on our mattress every Saturday. Few things feel as good as crawling in between clean sheets. That's what it felt like to me when I became a Christian. I felt clean inside. I've never doubted my decision to accept Christ.

How I Wound Up Becoming a Preacher in Retirement

Mustang Baptist Church is a little old church. When I was a kid, we lived in a house next door. I grew up in that church. Anyway, only about four people were still going there a few months ago. Most of the people had moved off or passed away. They were thinking about selling the church or giving it to somebody. But then Dale Redfearn, one of the members, said, "You're ordained, aren't you? You can preach." It wasn't really exactly what I wanted to do, but I felt like I was supposed to do it. Things have worked out real good. We've done a lot of work on the church. The most we've had in Sunday morning worship was 101. My whole family is coming, which has been a big blessing. We've had a couple of gospel singings on Saturday night, with ice cream-and-pie suppers. Boy, we had a bunch of people come out for those.

I spent a good while this morning trying to get my outline for next week's sermon. I get up and tell a lot of football stories. To me, being an athlete and being a Christian are a whole lot the same. You've got to have some discipline to do what you ought to do. I wear a tie when I preach. I'm old-fashioned. To me, it's sacred ground when you step into the pulpit. You don't need to get up there in flip-flops and a stringy shirt. I want the Lord to think I'm dressed special for Him.

Win-Loss Record Year-by-Year

— Bryson
1962: 5-5

— Pilot Point
1963: 6-3
1964: 7-3
1965: 8-1-2
1966: 5-5
1967: 5-4-1
1968: 10-1
1969: 8-2
1970: 7-3

56-22-3 – 8 years

— Celina
1972: 8-1-1
1973: 9-1
1974: 13-1-1 – tied Big Sandy, 0-0 for
                        Class B co-championship
1975: 13-1
1976: 9-1

52-5-2 – 5 years

— Pilot Point
1977: 7-3
1978: 9-1
1979: 11-1-1
1980: 14-0-1 – tied Tidehaven, 0-0 for
                        Class 2A co-championship
1981: 15-0   – beat Garrison, 32-0 for
                        Class 2A championship
1982: 12-1
1983: 11-1-1

1984:   10-1
1985:   13-1

102-9-3 – 9 years
— Sherman
1986:   6-4
1987:   6-4

12-8 – 2 years

— Celina
1988:   13-2
1989:   8-3
1990:   9-1-1
1991:   8-2
1992:   8-3
1993:   7-3
1994:   11-1
1995:   15-1   – beat Alto, 32-28 for
                Class 2A championship
1996:   11-1
1997:   11-3
1998:   14-2   – beat Elysian Fields, 21-0 for
                Class 2A, Division II championship
1999:   16-0   – beat Elysian Fields, 38-7 for
                Class 2A, Division II championship
2000:   16-0   – beat Mart, 21-17 for
                Class 2A, Division II championship
2001:   16-0   – beat Garrison, 41-35 for Class 2A,
                Division II championship
163-22-1 – 14 years

— Pilot Point
2002:   7-4
2003:   7-5
2004:   8-3

20-12 – 3 years

— Aubrey

2009:   11-2
2010:   4-6
2011:   4-6

19-14 – 3 years

<u>**Overall Record: 429-97-9 over 45 seasons**</u>

Acknowledgments

G.A. Moore deserves great credit for this book. He sat with me patiently for hour after hour, month after month, recalling the highlights of his career and his views on football strategy and player development. I'd also like to thank the members of Coach Moore's family for the generous amount of time they spent time with me. They are his wife, Lois Ann; daughters, Pam Moore, Tona Van-Hook-Drees, and Carol Lynn; and son, Gary Don Moore.

Outside of the family, coaches Butch Ford and Bill Elliott were extremely helpful in providing insights into Coach Moore's success. Both Ford and Elliott spent many years as assistants under Coach Moore at Celina High School before becoming head coaches themselves at the football powerhouse.

Dozens of former players under Coach Moore agreed to be interviewed for this book. Thank you all for sharing your memories. In particular, Steve Carey, Alvin Evans, Sonny Gibbs, Pat Hunn, Greg Pelzel, and Junior Worthey recounted anecdotes and impressions that brought Coach Moore to life.

I also owe a debt of gratitude Janet Harris, who adeptly shaped the manuscript and motivated me early on; my agent, John Monteleone, who found an outstanding publisher in Cardinal Publishers Group; and Tom Doherty and Morgan Sears with Cardinal for their vision in bringing the book to fruition.

Writing this book was a team project. Thanks to all the players.

References

Bynum, Mike, ed. 2003. *King Football: Greatest Moments in Texas High School Football History*. Columbus, OH: Epic Sports Classics.

Carver, John and Gordon Wood. 2001. *Coach of the Century, an Autobiography*. Dallas, TX: Hard Times Cattle Company Publishing.

Cashion, Ty. 1998. *Pigskin Pulpit: A Social History of Texas High School Football Coaches*. Austin, TX: Texas State Historical Association.

McMurray, Bill. 1985. *Texas High School Football*. Icarus Press.

Patoski, Joe Nick. 2011. *Texas High School Football: More Than a Game*. Austin, TX: Bob Bullock Texas State History Museum.

Smith, Dave, ed. 1999. *100 Years of Texas High School Football*. Dallas, TX: Dallas Morning News.